WILDLIFE PHOTOGRAPHER OF THE YEAR
PORTFOLIO one

PICTURE EDITOR: PETER WILKINSON FRPS
PROJECT CO-ORDINATOR: HELEN GILKS

FOUNTAIN PRESS

Fountain Press Limited
Queensborough House
2 Claremont Road
Surbiton
Surrey KT6 4QU
England

Art Direction by Nigel Osborne
Designed by Sally Stockwell
Typesetting by Midford Ltd, London W1

Reproduction and Printing by
Regent Publishing Services Ltd
Hong Kong

ISBN 0 86343 395 2

C O N T E N T S

FOREWORD

I first became involved in this prestigious competition at its very first exhibition in 1965. Since then, it has evolved in many ways. It has attracted more and more entries; it has introduced many new categories; and above all, it has established a world-wide reputation and become the centre of attention for wildlife photographers all around the world.

Getting any kind of picture of an animal that may be shy, rare or even dangerous, seems quite difficult enough to many of us who have tried it. But the judges of this competition have set standards of composition, lighting, framing and many other qualities that were once thought practical only for those taking pictures of people. In doing that, they have lifted wildlife picture-taking from little more than a cataloguing process to one of the great triumphs of the photographer's art.

That this should be so is surely no surprise. If you begin with nature and add art, then some great pictures must result. Here is the cream of more than 10,000 wildlife photographs that were entered for the 1991 competition. They are among the best in the world.

SIR DAVID ATTENBOROUGH

What you see in this book is a celebration of the natural world in a collection of memorable images – the first occasion that it has been possible to see together, in print, the 150 or so photographs that comprise a year's winning and commended entries to the Wildlife Photographer of the Year competition. And as a whole, this collection of images is surely proof that wildlife photography has reached the realms of mainstream art.

Elevating the status of wildlife photography has always been one of the aims of the contest, mainly because (and *despite* the seeming supremacy of moving pictures) still images can have tremendous impact and, therefore, usefulness when it comes to championing the natural world.

The contest was born in 1965, when popular nature conservation was a new idea and when BBC WILDLIFE Magazine was called *Animals*. As now, it was an international affair, reflecting the magazine's wide readership (now 1.3 million, in more than 80 countries), but with two sections – Britain and overseas – and three categories – Birds, Mammals, and All Others. The stated aim was to ''encourage the work of wildlife photographers and enhance the prestige of wildlife photography . . . and to benefit the animals themselves by creating greater public interest in them and that all-important topic – conservation.''

More than 500 entries were received, and David Attenborough presented a gold medal especially designed by Peter Scott to the overall winner – the Wildlife Photographer of the Year.

Sixteen years later, in 1981, the magazine added a competition for younger photographers and, for the first time, put on an exhibition of the commended and winning images. In 1984, three more significant things happened: the competition acquired a sponsor – Prudential Assurance; the magazine joined forces with the Natural History Museum – the ideal organisation to host a prestigious exhibition and provide a presentation venue; and an organiser, Helen Gilks, was appointed to oversee the smooth running of the event. This was also the year when the partnership was joined by the Fauna and Flora Preservation Society – the longest established conservation organisation in the world.

From then on, the competition was run at its present size, offering more than 40 major prizes in addition to two prestigious awards.

Each category was adopted by a presenter with, in most cases, special links to the subject and the organisers. Until his death in 1989, Sir Peter Scott, one of the great father figures of modern conservation, presented the two top awards: specially designed bronze trophies of a scarlet ibis, the bird which subsequently became the competition's logo. Presenters involved over the past eight years include Sir David Attenborough, Heather Angel, Chris Baines, David Bellamy, Dr Neil Chalmers, Nick Davies, Gerald Durrell, Lee Durrell, Eric Hosking, Anthony Huxley, Simon King, Richard Mabey, Virginia McKenna, Bill Oddie, Julian Pettifer, Andrew Sachs, Lady Scott, Keith Shackleton, Tony Soper and Ralph Steadman.

In 1990, British Gas joined forces with us, adding its name to the title and taking the role of overall sponsor, which it remains today, allowing us to run the competition at its current high level.

Last year, one of our greatest supporters, Eric Hosking, died. In his memory, and with the aim of encouraging new talent, we have introduced the Eric Hosking Award for the best portfolio presented by a young photographer aged 26 or under. The pictures by the first winner of this award can be seen on pages 37 to 44.

Over the past eight years, the number and quality of the entries have risen year by year, and the truly international flavour of the event can be seen by flicking through the pages of this book. More overseas entries come from the US than from any other country apart, of course, from the UK, and the significant number of winning images by US photographers has helped raise the standards of the competition.

Certainly, this collection of images can be said to fulfil the competition's current aims: ''To find the best wildlife pictures taken by photographers worldwide, and to emphasise through the work of such photographers the beauty, wonder and importance of the natural world.''

Rosamund Kidman Cox
EDITOR BBC WILDLIFE MAGAZINE

For more than 15 summers it has been my pleasure to join a judging panel of photographic aficionados to evaluate some of the finest wildlife photographs sent from all four corners of the globe. In the early days, judging of the Wildlife Photographer of the Year competition was modest enough in size to be easily accommodated at the home of the late Eric Hosking. Today, some 10,000 entries are submitted.

In order to tackle this huge contribution, two whole days are spent pre-judging at the BBC in Bristol. After a week's break, the full panel of judges meet at the Natural History Museum to spend one or two days assiduously working our way through the transparencies.

The panel of judges, most of whom have been with me for some years, provide a good balance of expertise and experience. They include Rosamund Kidman Cox, Editor of BBC WILDLIFE Magazine, Pedro Silmon, Art Editor of *The Sunday Times Magazine*, Bruce Pearson, artist and naturalist, and Giles Clarke, Head of Exhibition Planning at the Natural History Museum. This provides the essential continuity to judging the competition. It has, however, always been our policy to invite one or two additional judges to join us. For the 1991 competition, Amanda Nevill, Secretary of the Royal Photographic Society, brought a freshness and her own definite opinion to our deliberations. The judges look first and foremost for aesthetic appeal, and place an emphasis on photographs taken under wild and free conditions.

When confronted with so many superb images it can be painful to discard what we know has been a work of love, patience and endurance, but the fact that we nearly always reach a decision with unanimity and little dissent makes me confident that, in most cases, we make the correct judgement.

Since the first Wildlife Photographer of the Year competition in 1965, the top award has been given for a single image, and we open this book with the award-winning images from 1984 to 1990. But in 1991, the organising committee felt that the prestigious title of 'Wildlife Photographer of the Year' should be awarded for a portfolio. Frans Lanting, the photographer whose images won him the 1991 award, proved to be a worthy choice.

Bruce Coleman
CHAIRMAN, JUDGING PANEL

Since 1984, the Wildlife Photographer of the Year exhibition has become the annual winter highlight of The Natural History Museum's programme. The award ceremony is a splendid event with photographers from all over the world being presented with their prizes by a unique group of celebrities. There is no other occasion where so much talent in the field of wildlife photography is gathered together to celebrate the vitality of the natural world and the art of capturing it with the camera.

The exhibition that results each year from the competition is visited by many thousand members of the public during its stay in the Museum. it brings together all the winning photographs as well as the runners-up and more than 40 of the highly commended images. The other commended shots are shown in a slide-projection booth. The 1991 exhibition is on display at the Museum for five busy months and there are also two touring versions which visit a wide range of venues throughout the UK.

The Wildlife Photographer of the Year competition is a thoroughly international event and so it is appropriate that the 1991 exhibition will not only be seen and enjoyed in Britain, but will tour France, The Netherlands and Canada. It will also appear in Germany at the annual meeting of the German Nature Photographers Club.

Giles Clarke
HEAD OF EXHIBITION PLANNING,
THE NATURAL HISTORY
MUSEUM, LONDON

British Gas
WILDLIFE
PHOTOGRAPHER
OF·THE·YEAR
1991
COMPETITION

Organised by

B B C W I L D L I F E M A G A Z I N E
— *and* —

THE NATURAL HISTORY MUSEUM
—— *in association with* ——
The Fauna and Flora Preservation Society

Sponsored by

British Gas

RICHARD AND JULIA KEMP (UK)
GOOSANDER FISHING

"This shot was taken from a glass-fronted hide built into a river bank in Wester Ross, Scotland, while we were making a film about goosanders for Survival Anglia Television. The bird was one of a clutch of goosander ducklings which we hand-reared from eggs rescued at the time of the annual destruction of goosander nests, which occurs because of the birds' supposed effects on salmon stocks."

● *Nikon FE with 50mm lens; flash*

CHARLES G SUMMERS JR (USA)
YOUNG CHEETAH AND SPRINGBOK

"This is one of a sequence depicting a springbok falling victim to a female cheetah and her family. The mother had throttled the springbok and left it to her two cubs, whom she was teaching to hunt, to do the rest. But when one of the cubs straddled the victim, it suddenly revived, rising beneath its young attacker and taking it completely by surprise."

● *Nikon F2 with 400mm lens; f4 at 1/2000 sec; motor drive; Kodachrome 64*

RAJESH BEDI (INDIA)
HIMALAYAN BLACK BEAR (left)

"These bears are usually nocturnal, but it is sometimes possible to find one still at large just after sunrise. This individual was so intent on stripping bark off a sissoo tree in the Terai jungle of the Himalayan foothills that I was able to get several frames before it noticed me."

● *Nikon FM with 80-200mm lens; f4.5 at 1/250 sec; Kodachrome 64*

JONATHAN SCOTT (UK)
WILD DOG IMMOBILISING WILDEBEEST

"I was watching a pack of wild dogs chase a wildebeest in the Serengeti National Park when one of the adult males grabbed the animal's upper lip – an action that helps immobilise the prey animal, perhaps because the upper lip and nose region has a rich nerve centre. I knew straight away that it was a 500mm shot. The area of real drama involved the animals' heads, and by getting tight in on the action I emphasised the most basic of all struggles – the struggle for life between predator and prey."

● *Canon F1 with 500mm lens; f4.5; Kodachrome 64 rated at 80 ISO*

JIM BRANDENBURG (USA)
GEMSBOK AND SAND DUNES

"Food and water are hard to come by in the Namibian sand dunes, which are the tallest in the world, and the gemsbok survives by eating just about any vegetation it can find, digging for tubers when nothing else is available. This image emphasises the harshness of the terrain which the animal inhabits."

● *Nikon F3 with 200mm lens; f8 at 1/125 sec; Kodachrome 64*

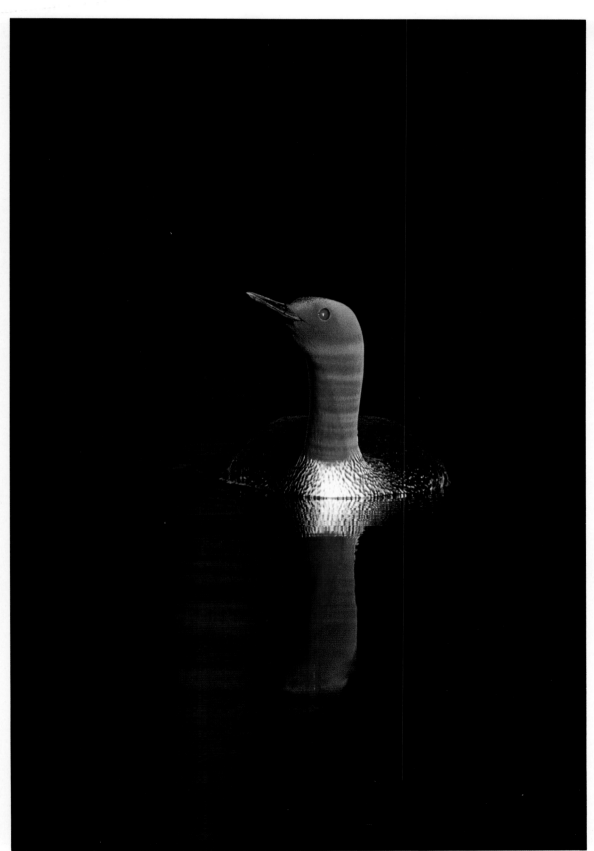

JOUNI RUUSKANEN (FINLAND)
RED-THROATED DIVER

"I have been studying red-throated divers in Finland for more than 20 years and photographing them whenever I can. On this occasion it was already getting dark when suddenly the sun peeked out from behind the clouds and gave a beautiful and unusual light on the bird."

● *Nikon FM with 560mm lens; f6.8 with 1/50 sec; Kodachrome 64*

WENDY SHATTIL (USA)
RED FOX CUB

"The owners of a property on which some fox cubs were located invited me to photograph the cubs. One of the young was particularly inquisitive. Whenever I set up for an afternoon of photographing, he was invariably the first to appear. At times I think he was intrigued by his reflection in the large glass element of my 800mm lens. On the day this photo was taken, a spot of late afternoon light appeared as the cub settled into the tall grass near its den."

● *Canon T90 with 800mm lens; f6.7 at 1/250 sec; Fujichrome 50*

FRANS LANTING (THE NETHERLANDS)

Frans Lanting's winning portfolio of pictures were all taken in the Okavango Delta in Botswana. Altogether, he spent almost a year in the Okavango on assignment for *National Geographic* to document not only the wildlife but also the interactions between man and nature in the area.

After taking a Master's degree in environmental economics in his native Holland, Frans moved to the USA and took up photography. He is totally self taught, both as a photographer and as a naturalist. In the mid-80s he started an association with *National Geographic* which has taken him to some of the wildest and remotest places on Earth —

Madagascar, the Falklands and South Georgia, the Hawaiian and the Galapagos Islands.

Frans uses Nikon equipment but does not make a note of technical details, which is why this information is not included in the picture captions.

IMPALA

"To most tourists impala are just an antelope they'd rather pass up in favour of finding lions or leopards. But to me they are a never-ending source of inspiration. I took the picture at a particular waterhole I went to each morning. This is one of the keys to my photography — becoming a fixture in the landscape so that the animals take me for granted."

ZEBRAS PANIC

"Zebras are quite nervous by nature. They approach water very cautiously and, at the slightest sense of disturbance, real or imagined, panic ripples through the herd."

WINNING PORTFOLIO

BULLFROG DEFENDING ITS RAIN POOL

"This picture symbolises the onset of the rainy season. The bullfrog had been hibernating or, rather, aestivating for most of the year and had just come back to life with the arrival of the rains."

WINNING PORTFOLIO

FAN FISHING (below)

"Black egrets engage in a peculiar fishing technique — fanning out their wings to shade the water from glare. It is quite a common sight in Okavango but not easy to photograph in this way."

SAD REFLECTION

"This photo is part of my coverage of human ecology – the zebra was killed by the trophy hunters (reflected in the animal's eye) under a licensed sport-hunting programme. Hunting is very much part of life in the Okavango and trophy hunting contributes a lot of money to the local economy."

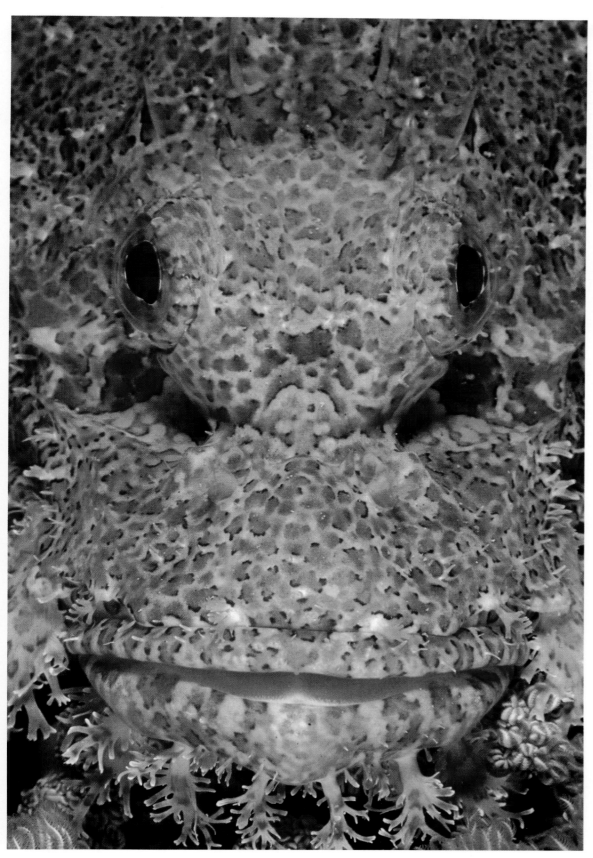

BURT JONES & MAURINE SHIMLOCK (USA)

Burt Jones and Maurine Shimlock are a husband-and-wife underwater photographic team based in Texas. For ten years until 1987 they owned a small dive operation on Mexico's Caribbean coast. When overdevelopment threatened the barrier reef along the coast they became interested in underwater photography as a way of recording the rapidly changing underwater environment. Since then they have worked in the Solomon Islands, Red Sea, Fiji, Borneo, Vanuatu and New Zealand and continue to be amazed at the complexity of life found in the seas.

SCORPIONFISH FACE

"Scorpionfish are so sure of the strength of their venom and the success of their camouflage that they rarely move, even when approached by divers. This portrait shows the feathery appendages and mottled colour that help make this fish a master of disguise. Only its eyes and mouth distinguish it from the Red Sea coral."

● *Nikon F3 with 90mm lens; underwater housing; strobes; f11 at 1/60 sec; Kodachrome 25*

BAR JACKS OVER REEF CREST

"Ascending from a late afternoon dive in Belize, we were surrounded momentarily by this feeding school of juvenile jacks. These fish are often attracted to divers and perhaps feed on tiny organisms trapped by their air bubbles."

● *Nikon F3 with 15mm lens; underwater housing; strobes; f8 at 1/60 sec; Fujichrome 100*

GREY SHARK (below)

"This photo was taken at the exit of an underwater tunnel in the Solomon Islands. Most of the Solomons were formed by volcanic activity and the fissure in this island provided the perfect frame for a grey whaler shark as it patrolled the blue seas."

● *Nikonos III with 15mm lens; f5.6 at 1/60 sec; Fujichrome 100*

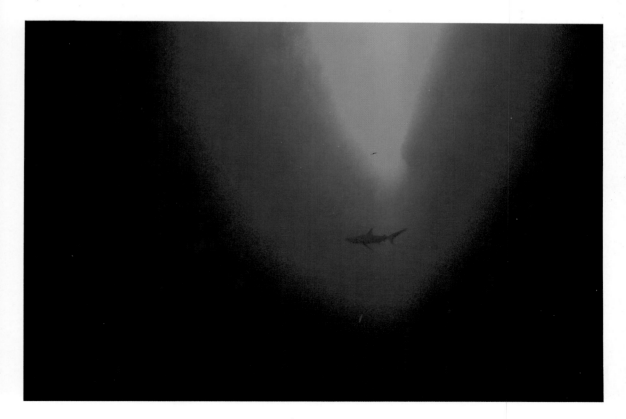

RUNNER-UP PORTFOLIO

PORKFISH SCHOOL, BELIZE

"Schools of fish often move as one to better defend themselves or to capture prey. This school was diving in unison near the surface and made a perfect natural-light subject."

● *Nikon F3 with 55mm lens; underwater housing; f8 at 1/60 sec; Fujichrome 50*

RUNNER-UP PORTFOLIO

FILEFISH FIN DETAIL (right)

"When we saw this file fish we were immediately struck by the incredible patterns near the base of its tail and got close enough for this one shot."

● *Nikon F3 with 90mm lens; underwater housing; strobes; f11 at 1/60 sec; Fujichrome 50*

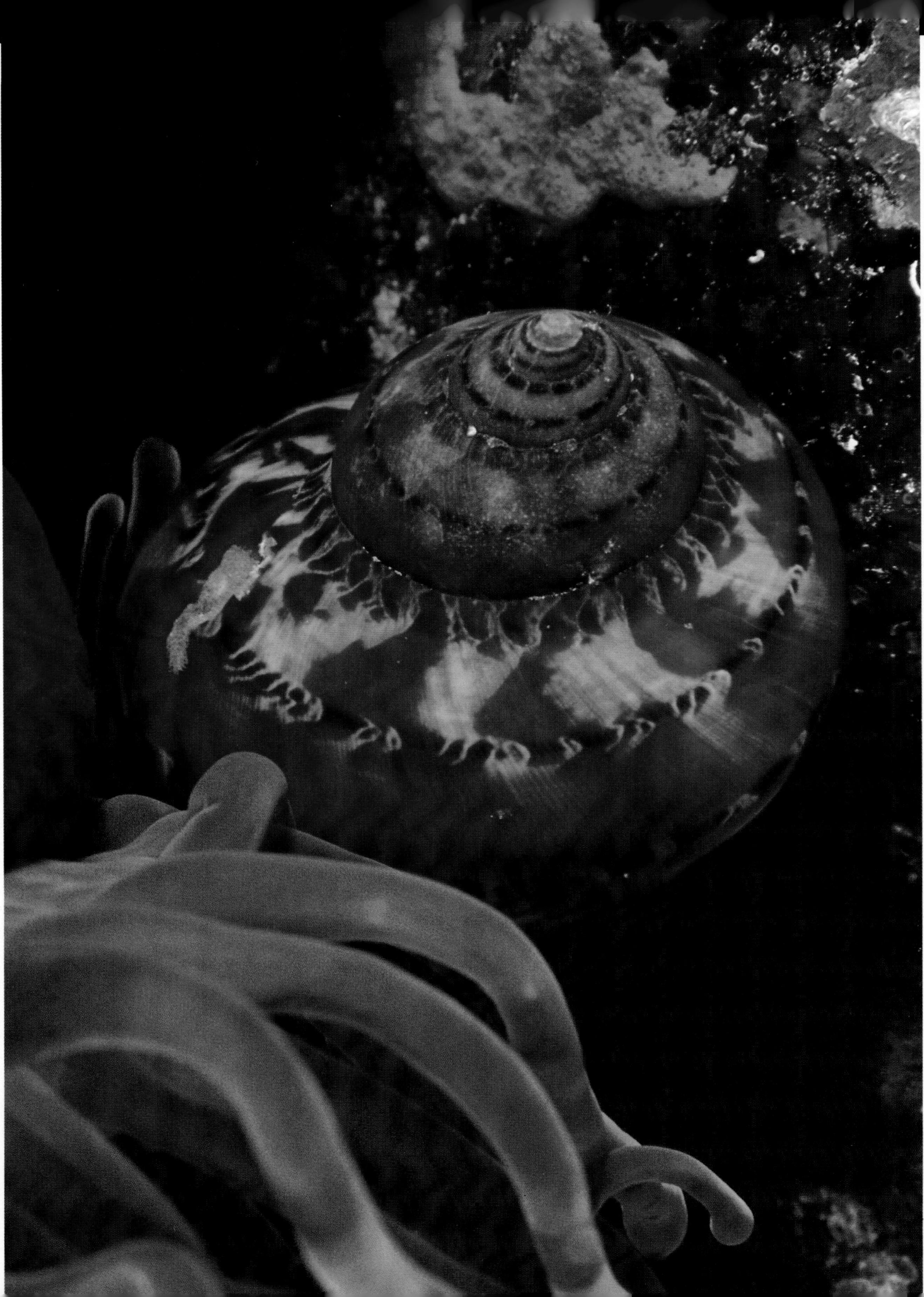

STILL LIFE WITH TURBAN SHELL, RED SEA (left)

''Turbans, like most shells, are nocturnal and hide in holes in the reef during daylight. This one was spending the day nestling in the skirt of a carpet anemone. We were photographing anemonefish when a gust of current lifted the anemone, revealing the shell.''

● *Nikon F3 with 90mm lens; underwater housing; strobes; f8 at 1/60 sec; Kodachrome 25*

ANEMONE MOUTH DETAIL

''These invertebrates come in all shapes, sizes and colours, but the carpet anemones of the Indo-Pacific have the most unusual patterns. As the animal was feeding, the fleshy parts of the mouth unfolded and reminded us of the petals of an exotic flower.''

● *Nikon F3 with 90mm lens; underwater housing; strobes; f16 at 1/60 sec; Fujichrome 50*

LIONFISH

"Lionfish are difficult to photograph because they turn and present their poisonous dorsal spines when approached too closely. We came upon this group off the Solomon Islands, and were able to get close in for a wide-angle shot because they were feeding in a strong current and more interested in the swirling baitfish than our presence."

● *Nikonos V with 15mm lens; strobes; f8 at 1/60 sec; Fujichrome 100*

ANEMONE EVISCERATING (right)

"Most anemones have only their stinging tentacles as defensive weapons, but this particular species offers part of itself as a subterfuge. The idea is that a predator will attack this easily regenerated material and leave the rest of the anemone's body alone."

● *Nikon F3 with 90mm lens; underwater housing; strobes; f22 at 1/60 sec; Fujichrome 50*

KONRAD WOTHE (GERMANY)

Konrad Wothe is a professional wildlife film cameraman and photographer. He has travelled widely and his portfolio includes shots from Madagascar, Russia, Hungary, Galapagos and Canada.

AERIAL SHOT OF PECHORA-ILYCH RESERVE

''In September 1990, I was working for a film project about nature reserves in the USSR and had the opportunity to take some aerial shots from a helicopter, flying over the Pechora-Ilych reserve in the Urals. It was a marvellous sight – untouched taiga as far as the eye could see.''

● *Canon T90; f4 at 1/500 sec; Fujichrome Velvia*

GOLDEN BAMBOO-LEMUR

"While I was filming for *Jungle Spirits of Madagascar* Bernard Meier who discovered the golden bamboo-lemur in 1986, led us into the rainforest of Ranomafana. There we finally found the lemurs and I was able to take this shot of a male eating a piece of bamboo."

● *Canon T90 with 300mm lens; flash; f4; Fujichrome 100*

RUNNER-UP PORTFOLIO

GREAT BUSTARD COURTSHIP DISPLAY
"Great bustards still live in the vast puszta plains of Hungary, but photographing these shy birds in the open is not easy. I was lucky, and found the display area of this male bird near a thicket of trees, where I was able to set up a hide. I could only leave the hide when it was dark, and it was more than a week before the bird came within shooting distance."

● *Canon T90 with 800mm lens; tripod; f5.6 at 1/250 sec; Fujichrome 100*

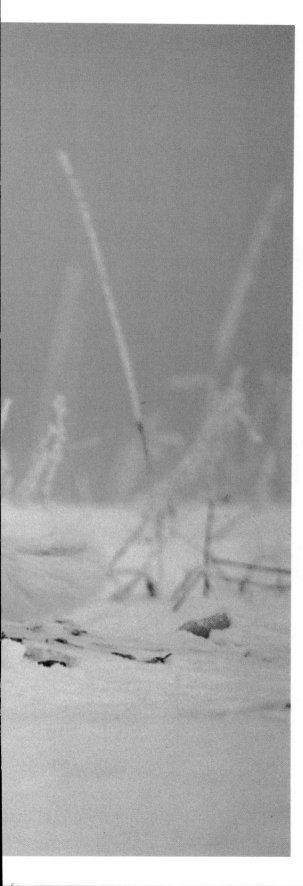

ARCTIC FOX (left)
"This arctic fox was quite tame. I found it in an area busy with tundra buggies full of tourists watching polar bears."
● *Canon EOS1 with 80-200mm zoom lens; f4 at 1/250 sec; Fujichrome Velvia*

RED FOXES FIGHTING (right)
"While in Churchill, Canada, we saw red foxes every day beside the road. We discovered that one pair had a den in one of the dunes and a little later a small fight broke out between them."
● *Canon EOS1 with 300mm lens and x2 extender; f2.8 at 1/350 sec; Fujichrome 100*

RED FOXES (above)
"These foxes are enjoying the last rays of sun of the day. This marvellous scene attracted half a dozen photographers who set up their tripods in a semi-circle some 60 metres away. Surprisingly, the foxes didn't take much notice of them."
● *Canon EOS1 with 300mm lens; monopod; f2.8 at 1/250 sec; Fujichrome 100*

ARCTIC FOX (left)
"The arctic fox is difficult to spot in its snowy surroundings. I found this individual resting."
● *Canon T90 with 150-600 zoom lens; monopod; f8 at 1/500 sec; Fujichrome 100*

RUNNER-UP PORTFOLIO

PARSON'S CHAMELEON

"Chameleons are slow-moving but well-camouflaged creatures. Once you have found one, you have the time to take a close look at its wonderful, independently mobile eyes."

● *Canon T90 with 90mm macro lens; flash; f16; Fujichrome 100*

RUNNER-UP PORTFOLIO

SALLY LIGHTFOOT CRAB (left)

"This crab was feeding on an urchin, and as I approached it with my 300mm lens the crab squirted water to scare me away."

● *Canon EOS600 with 300mm lens; f4.5; flash; Fujichrome 100*

POLAR BEAR WALKING ON ICE

"Every November, hundreds of polar bear gather in the Churchill area, waiting for Hudson Bay to freeze over. Only from the ice can they hunt their main food source, ringed seals. From a tundra buggy I was able to photograph these two bears walking on the first ice."

● *Canon EOS1 with 300mm lens; f4.5 at 1/250 sec; window mount; Fujichrome Velvia*

NEIL MCINTYRE (UK)

The Eric Hosking Award was introduced in 1991 and is awarded for the best portfolio of pictures (up to a maximum of 10) submitted by a photographer aged 26 or under. The award is in memory of Eric Hosking who was probably Britain's most famous wildlife photographer and a supporter of this competition since its inception in 1965.

The winner, 25-year-old Neil McIntyre, comes from the Highlands of Scotland. As a young boy he was fascinated by the wildlife around him, and at the age of 16 he acquired his first camera. He has had no formal training in photography and says that he has learned mainly from his mistakes.

ROE DEER IN MARSHLAND

"I have regularly seen roe deer moving about in the reeds on marshland just a short distance from my home. I felt that soft evening light would suit the scene best, but it was not until the third attempt that a roe deer appeared in an open enough clearing to photograph it. Even then it stopped only for a second, just enough time for one frame."

● *Canon T90 with 400mm lens; tripod; f11 at 1/125sec; Kodachrome 64*

MOUNTAIN HARE (left)

"From past experience, I have found the best way to get close to mountain hares is to look for one lying in the heather – they seem to prefer to stay hidden rather than run off. On this occasion I spotted the tips of its ears and crawled to within five metres of it. I focused on its ears and made a squeaking sound. Immediately the hare sat up, and I released the shutter."

● *Canon T90 with 400mm lens; tripod; f8 at 1/250 sec; Kodachrome 64*

RED SQUIRREL

"Finding a large number of eaten pine cones scattered below a Scots pine tree, I thought it likely that a squirrel was feeding there regularly. I put up a hide on a steep bank level with the lower branches, and on my first visit was lucky enough to see a squirrel eating cones, at first high in the tree, then on the lower branches."

● *Canon T90 with 400mm lens; f4 at 1/30 sec; Kodachrome 64*

ROTHIEMURCHUS (below)

"This is one of the last remnants of the Caledonian pine forest. I was in the forest during the rutting season looking for stags when I noticed the scene in the distance, with mist hanging low around the old trees. It seemed to sum up the haunting frozen-in-time atmosphere of the old forests."

● *Canon T90 with 400mm lens; tripod; f11 at 1/30 sec; Kodachrome 64*

GLEN ETIVE

"The picture illustrates many features of the Highland landscape – the high mountains, the glen and the small loch, with a dull but atmospheric sky, typical of many Highland days. I used a low viewpoint to emphasise the moss-covered stones in the foreground."

● *Canon T90 with 35mm lens; tripod; f16 at 1/15sec; Fujichrome Velvia 50*

AWARD PORTFOLIO

RAVEN LANDING

"I was looking for white hares when I noticed this dead Scots pine silhouetted against the Cairngorms. Every so often a raven would land on it to preen itself. I got into a suitable position, focused the lens and waited for one to land."

● *Canon T90 with 400mm lens; tripod; f8 at 1/500sec; Kodachrome 64*

AWARD PORTFOLIO

BOG BEAN

"A small boat was needed to get to the bog bean plants, which were in a sheltered part of the loch. After setting up my equipment I had to wait for a suitable break in the wind, so that the reflection would be in calm water and so that the boat would be still during the exposure."

● *Canon T90 with 90mm macro lens; tripod; f11 at 1/15 sec; Fujichrome 100*

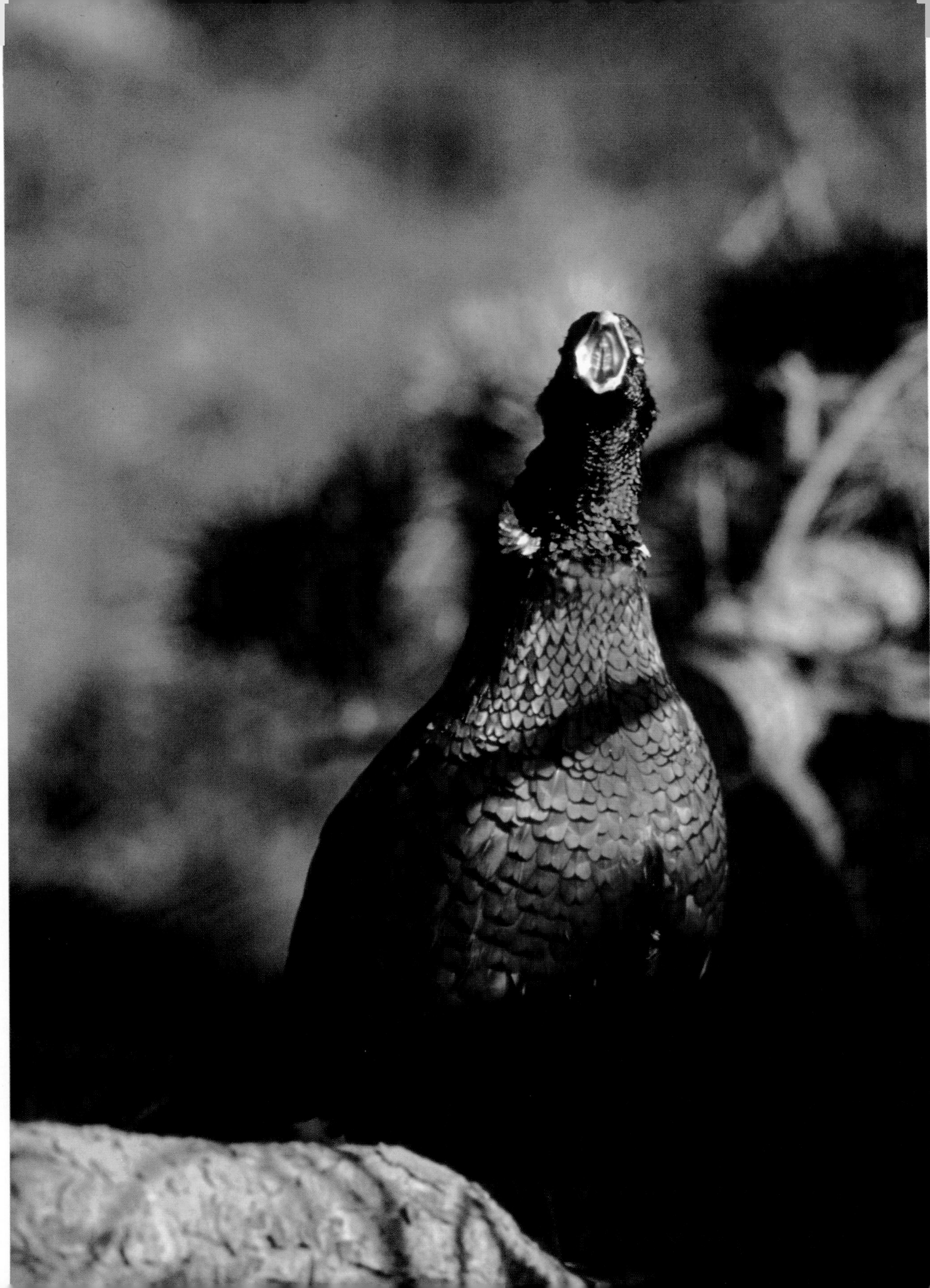

PHEASANT CALLING (left)

"The pheasant was displaying by a wood and appeared to be moving along its edge. Anticipating its direction, I crept round to a suitable position well in front of the bird and concealed myself in some bushes. The pheasant came right up to me and obligingly called out. Being so close, it heard the shutter and retreated along the woodland edge. But one shot was enough."

● *Canon T90 with 400mm lens; tripod; f5.6 at 1/250 sec; Fujichrome 100*

TAWNY OWL

"I had seen an owl several times on this tree in the early morning, and because it was beside a rough track, I decided to use my jeep as a hide. As the owl landed, the morning sun broke through the trees, giving the perfect opportunity for a picture."

● *Canon T90 with 400mm lens; bean bag; f4 at 1/15 sec; Fujichrome 100*

RED DEER STAGS BOXING (below)

"In spring, when casting their antlers, stags occasionally rise up on their hind legs to box, behaviour I had wanted to capture for some time. You can usually anticipate when it is going to happen, as the stags tend to size each other up for a few seconds before rising up. These few seconds are vital for getting the lens focused."

● *Canon T90 with 400mm lens; tripod; f8 at 1/500 sec; Kodachrome 64*

STEFAN MEYERS (GERMANY)
BOXING HARES

"In spring during the mating season, groups of hares gather in open meadows. Males attack each other, trying to hold their ground against rivals to mate with the females, and females box with males if they are not ready to mate. They stand on their hind feet trying to keep their bodies far enough away from each other to avoid getting hurt by their opponent's sharp claws. It is difficult to get close enough to photograph these rituals and in the end I used a car."

● *Canon F1 with 800mm lens; f5.6 at 1/250 sec; Fujichrome 100*

ALAIN SAUNIER (SWITZERLAND)
ROE DEER
"One cold December morning, after trying unsuccessfully to photograph chamois, I returned to my car to take pictures of the frozen landscapes and trees while the sun was still low in the sky. Suddenly a roe deer buck came slowly out of the forest but when it saw two men with a dog in the distance, it leapt away. I got this picture on its third jump — the result of luck and the reflexes of an old photographer!"

● *Pentax LX with 300mm lens and 1.4x converter; monopod; f5.6; Kodachrome 64*

JUDD COONEY (USA)
MUTUAL GROOMING

"The early morning light was superb and the expression on the animals' faces engaging – mutual grooming is a common trait in whitetail deer."

● *Nikon F3 with 400mm lens; tripod; f8 at 1/125sec; Kodachrome 200*

HIGHLY COMMENDED

LAURIE CAMPBELL (UK)

RAIN-SOAKED DOE (right)

"This is one of a small herd of red deer that had been lying down, chewing the cud in pouring rain. One by one, they all stood up, and began shaking the water off themselves." Professional photographer Laurie Campbell concentrates on capturing the landscapes and wildlife of his native Scotland. He took this picture from a vehicle in Deeside.

● *Nikon F3 with 600mm lens; f5.6 at 1/15sec; Kodachrome 200*

HIGHLY COMMENDED

GERTRUD & HELMUT DENZAU (GERMANY)

SAMBAR DEER AND CROW

"We were in the Sariska Tiger Reserve and had spent the night in a hide overlooking a waterhole. Many animals appeared in the early morning, including this young sambar. The crow is interested in the scent glands, possibly to get at any ticks. The sambar was very accommodating and even allowed the crow to sit on his head."

● *Nikon F3 with 300mm lens; tripod; f5.6 at 1/125 sec; Kodachrome 64*

JOHN W WARDEN (USA)
RED FOX WITH PREY

"As a wildlife photographer I spend a lot of time in Denali National Park, Alaska. On this occasion I noticed a red fox walking along a road with an arctic ground squirrel and willow ptarmigan in its mouth. It showed no fear at all, and went right by me, heading back to its den. I took the picture with an auto-focus lens, tracking the animal as it approached."

● *Nikon F4s with 300mm lens; f4 at 1/500 sec; Fujichrome 100*

Rick McIntyre (USA)

MORE THAN A MOUTHFUL

"It was late July, in Denali National Park in Alaska, and this fox was more concerned about feeding its cubs than about me hiding behind the car. It was carrying three ground squirrels when suddenly it stopped, put them down, and stared intently to one side. It made a rush and within a second had caught and killed yet another squirrel. What took time was figuring out how to jam all four into its mouth."

● *Minolta Maxxum 900 with 300mm lens; f2.8 at 1/250 sec; Fujichrome 50*

FRANCISCO MÁRQUEZ (SPAIN)
WILD GOAT WITH ITS KID

"The Spanish wild goat inhabits remote mountainous regions. I followed this female on foot in the Gredos mountains for several hours and then, hiding behind rocks, I was able to photograph her and her kid as it stretched and playfully tested out its little horns."

● *Nikon F4s with 500mm lens; tripod; f5.6 at 1/350 sec; Kodachrome 64*

RICH KIRCHNER (USA)
SALMON FEAST (left)

"I saw these two six-month old grizzly cubs every day during a six-day stay near the Brooks River in Katmai National Park, Alaska. They were very interesting and playful and gave some great photo opportunities. Here the young bears were wading around in the water grabbing dead, or near dead, salmon floating downstream after spawning."

● *Nikon F4 with 500mm lens; tripod; f4 at 1/125 sec; Fujichrome Professional 100 pushed one stop to 200 ISO*

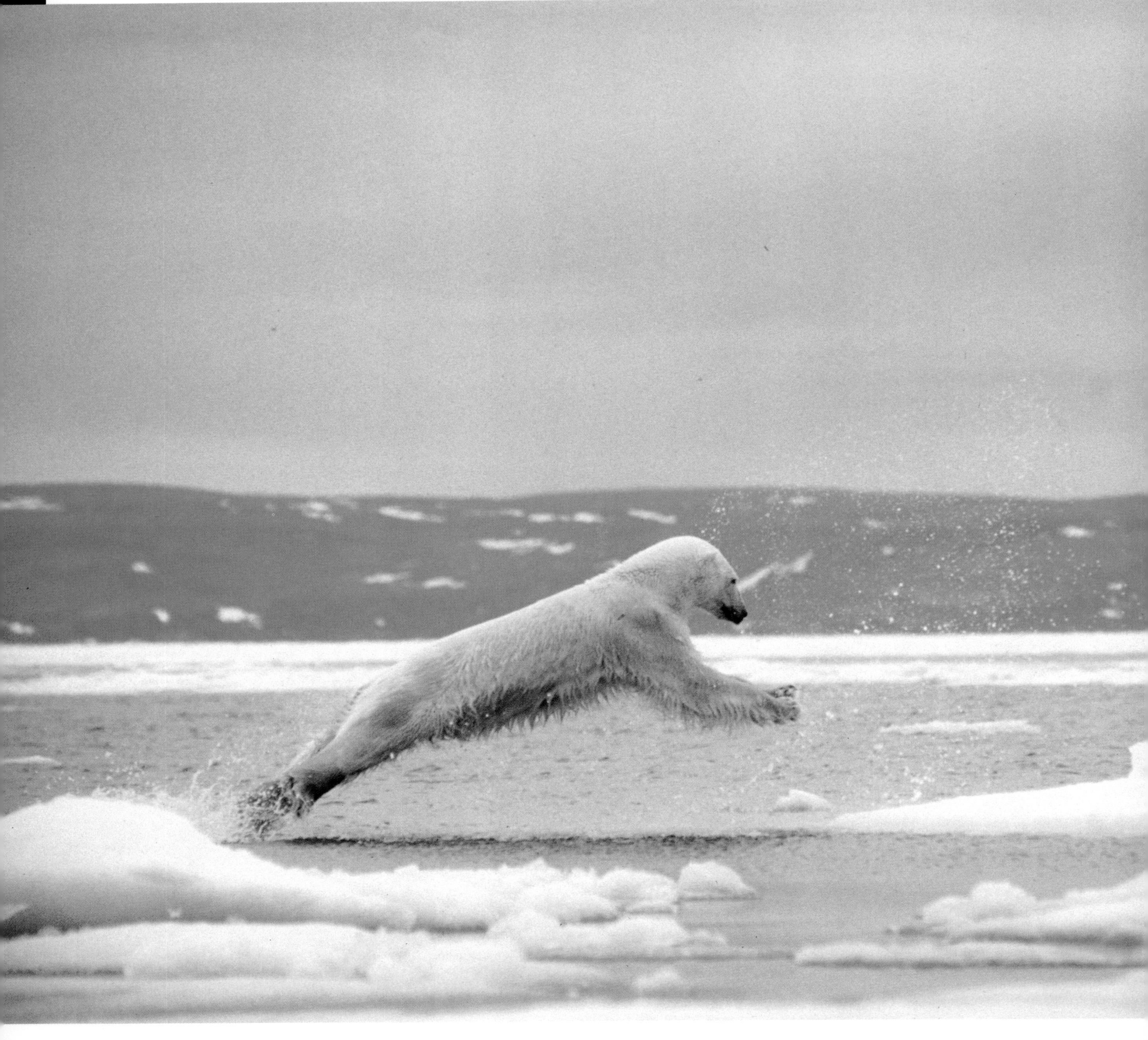

BOB GLOVER (UK)
HARE STRETCHING

"During the summer I set up two small hides to photograph hares on an area of waste ground near my home in Essex. People with dogs are usually bad news when taking pictures, but on this occasion they worked to my advantage driving this young hare close to my hide. It crouched low in the grass, staying there for a long time even after the danger had passed. Then it stood up, calmly stretched itself in front of my camera, and walked off."

● *Nikon FM2 with 600mm lens; f5.6 at 1/250 sec; Kodachrome 64*

DANIEL J COX (USA)
POLAR BEAR LEAPING (left)

"I was up in the North West Territories of Canada, close to the Arctic Circle, photographing polar bears as part of a calendar assignment. I hadn't seen a single bear so when we came upon this one, leaping from floe to floe, it was just pure excitement. People were getting in the way in the boat and I was thinking that you don't often get a chance to take a shot like this."

● *Nikon F4 with 80-200mm zoom lens; f8 at 1/250 sec; Kodachrome 64*

GLENN J PRATT (USA)
GRIZZLY COURTSHIP

"I have observed and photographed these two bears – Diver and Petite – since 1978 . . . The scene in this photograph was preceded by 15 minutes of foreplay in the icy waters of Brooks River. Diver then led Petite out of the river onto the road and attempted to mate. Rejected, Diver turned to face Petite, standing eight feet tall on his hind legs. Vocalizing softly, Petite stood up facing Diver and playfully shoved his chest with her forepaw. After a while the bears mated".

● *Nikon 8008 with 300mm lens; monopod; f3.5 at 1/250 sec; Kodachrome 64 rated at 80 ISO*

GLENN J PRATT (USA)
GRIZZLY PROTECTS CUBS

"Large grizzly males frequently kill cubs during the mating season. Here a grizzly sow is ferociously threatening a large male, warning it not to come any closer to her cubs." The shot was taken in the McNeil River State Game Sanctuary in Alaska, where every July large numbers of grizzlies concentrate along the river for salmon.

● *Nikon F4 with 300mm lens; tripod; f4 at 1/125 sec; Kodachrome 64 rated at 80 ISO*

KONRAD WOTHE (GERMANY)
SLEEPING POLAR BEAR

"When a blizzard or heavy snowfall closes in, polar bears often lie down in a snowbank and wait for better weather. I was well protected, sitting in a tundra buggy taking pictures with a 600mm lens out of the window."

● *Canon T90 with 150-600mm zoom lens; window mount; f5.6 at 1/250 sec; Fujichrome 100*

DANIEL J COX (USA)
SLEEPING BLACK BEAR

"The bear is sleeping in a swamp using a cedar tree for a pillow. I followed him there in the north woods of Minnesota and watched him sleep for six hours. Heavy autumn rain is saturating him and everything around him."

● *Nikon F4 with 80-200mm zoom lens; Kodachrome 64*

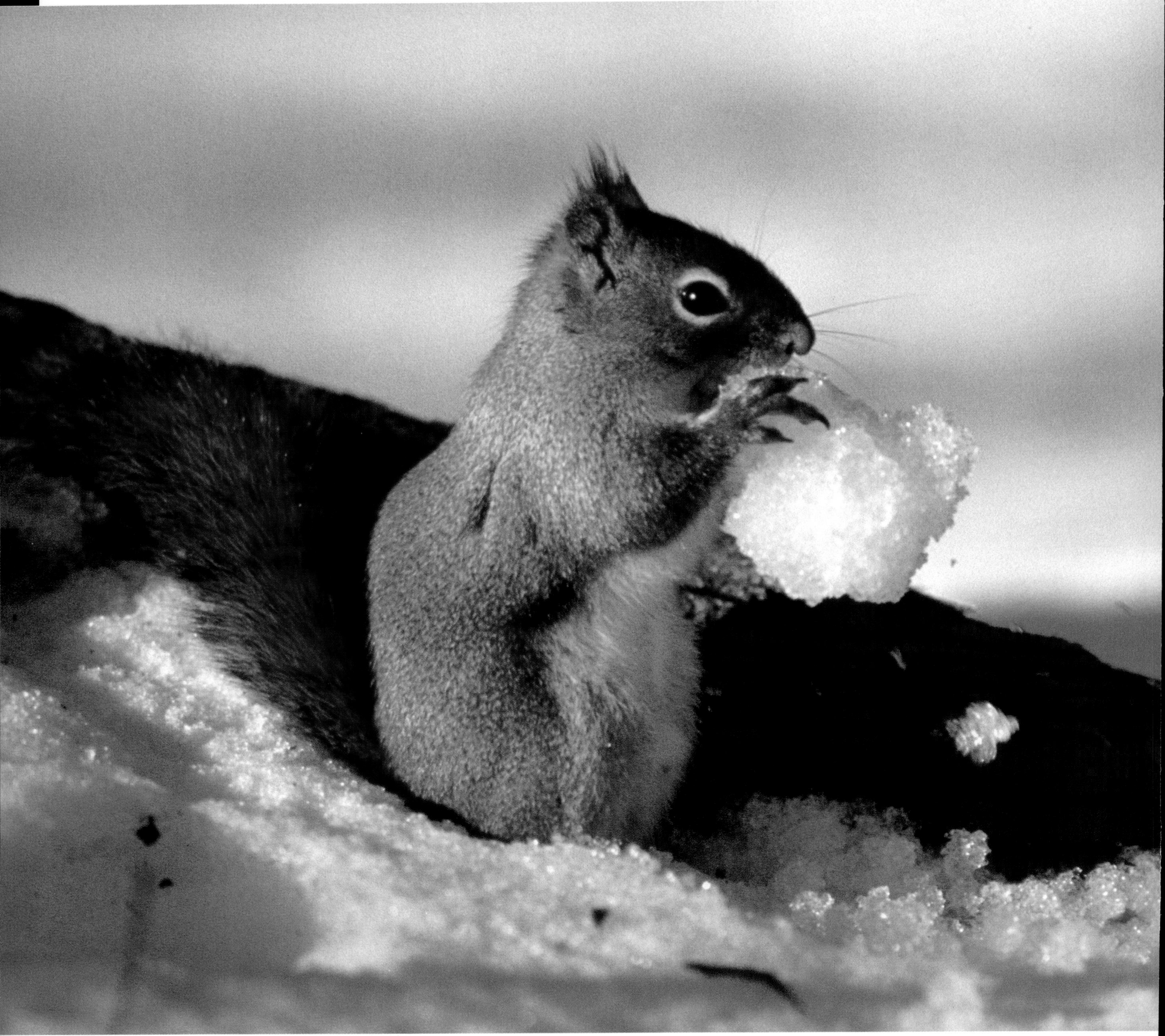

JUSSI MURTOSAARI (FINLAND)
RED SQUIRREL

"In 1990 there were more spruce cones than in any year since 1940 and squirrels were quite common. I took this photo in Jyvaskyla. I think that the squirrel looks quite funny with the cone in its mouth, almost as if it is smoking a cigar."

● *Nikon F3 with 300mm lens; f2.8 at 1/250 sec; Kodachrome 200*

JANET HAAS (USA)
RED SQUIRREL (left)

"This picture was taken early one cold sunny morning in Kensington Metro Park, Michigan. I was trying to get a shot of the squirrel perched on a tree root when unexpectedly he grabbed a chunk of snow in his front paws and started gnawing at it, apparently for the water."

● *Nikon 8008 with 300mm lens; tripod; f5.6 at 1/500 sec; Fujichrome 100*

NORBERT ROSING (GERMANY)
POLAR BEAR

"This mother polar bear is just launching into an attack on another bear who has come too close to her and her cub. I took the picture in Churchill, Canada, where I go regularly to take wildlife pictures."

● *Leica R6 with 280mm lens and 1.4 extender; f8 at 1/250 sec; Kodachrome 25*

LEV WEISMAN (USSR)
POLAR BEAR IN ITS DEN (right)

"I joined a group of scientists travelling to the east of Wrangel island where several hundred female polar bears make their dens. The ice was beginning to thaw, and the bears were starting to come out of their dens with their cubs. We spotted this female as she retreated back into her den and I started to walk closer, telling myself not to be frightened. The bear watched me from her den. Her nose quivered but I was convinced that she had accepted me. I focused my lens, all the time trying to forget that my life was in danger."

HELMUT PUM (AUSTRIA)

NEST THIEF

"I was sitting in the car at six o'clock in the morning when my attention was caught by starlings fluttering excitedly in front of a large woodpecker's hole. A pine marten appeared and proceeded to raid the starlings' nest, which was in the hole. I moved closer with my photo equipment but when the marten came out with a captured starling I was so excited that I forgot to switch my camera on. Luckily it went back into the hole again and I was able to take some pictures."

● *Canon T90 with 150-600 zoom lens; tripod; f5.6 at 1/15 sec*

BENJAMIN PÖNTINEN (FINLAND)

BLACK WOODPECKER

"To get this photograph I spent several hours a day in April perched on the same level as the woodpecker, seven metres up a ladder leaning on a spruce tree. I went to the forest at Lapua, in southern Finland, five times during the two weeks it took the male to dig the hole (the female coming by regularly to approve his work), but only on the last day did it snow."

● *Canon EOS10 with 300mm lens; Fujichrome 100*

GORDON COURT (NEW ZEALAND)
SKUAS AND ADELIE PENGUIN CHICKS

"About two hundred polar skuas nest in association with the Adelie penguins of the Northern Rookery at Cape Bird on Ross Island, Antarctica. Although most skuas subsist on a diet of fish, some, like those in the photo, are specialists at taking penguin eggs and chicks. The skuas must work in pairs to be successful – invariably, the larger female (on the right) will reach in with her bill and pull a chick clear. Some chicks are capable of defending themselves – the chick left of centre is in a classic defence posture and about to retaliate with its flippers."

● *Pentax ME Super with 300mm lens; tripod; hide; f4 at 1/125 sec; Kodachrome 64*

RISTO PETÄJÄMÄKI (FINLAND)
CAPERCAILLIE (left)

"Last spring, during the capercaillie mating season, I spent many mornings trying to get a photograph of this particular male at a lek near my home in eastern Finland. The morning I took this shot, I felt the lighting was just right."

● *Canon T70 with 200mm lens; tripod; f2.8 at 1/30 sec; Fujichrome 50*

BENOÎT RENEVEY (SWITZERLAND)
GREAT CRESTED GREBES (left)
"I have taken more than 500 photos of the breeding behaviour of great crested grebes over the past five years, spending more than 120 hours in a hide built on the water. The two birds here are in a rare phase of courtship display known as the penguin dance. This happens when the birds are very excited."

● *Canon F1 with 500mm lens; tripod; f4.5 at 1/500 sec; Kodachrome 64*

FRANS LANTING
(THE NETHERLANDS)
YELLOW-BILLED STORK
"The yellow-billed stork is carrying nest material back to the colony on an island deep in the Okavango delta. Falling water levels make fishing for their offspring easier at this time of year."

JEAN-FRANÇOIS HELIO (FRANCE) & NICOLAS VAN INGEN (THE NETHERLANDS)

KESTREL WITH PREY

"We photographed this scene of predation from a hide that we had built under a tree in order to photograph courtship kestrel display. At the time, we were watching and photographing kestrels in La Brenne, France."

● *Nikon FE2 with 400mm lens; tripod; f3.5 at 1/125 sec; Kodachrome 200*

KARL AMMANN (SWITZERLAND)

GROUND HORNBILL (right)

"This ground hornbill regularly sits on the roadside near Mount Kenya Game Ranch showing off its most recent captives – mainly rodents or frogs."

● *Nikon F4 with 80-200mm lens; Fujichrome Velvia*

GORDON LANGSBURY (UK)
WHITE-THROATED BEE-EATERS

"We were driving through Samburu Game Reserve in Kenya when I spotted two white-throated bee-eaters displaying to each other on a branch close to the ground. Afraid that they might fly off, I opted for my 600mm lens and managed a couple of frames with the sun shining through their wings before the birds flew off. Even though the sun was shining it was raining – the kind of conditions that can make an ordinary photograph spectacular."

● *Nikon F4 with 600mm lens; f5.6 auto; Kodachrome 200*

LENNART MELLGREN (SWEDEN)

RAVENS

"The photo was taken near the mountains of Halleberg during a freezing February snowstorm. To photograph shy birds such as ravens I go into my hide before daylight with lots of warm clothes and food. When I took this photo it was so cold that the bait I had put out to feed the birds had frozen hard. These ravens just sat in the trees with the wind and snow howling around them."

● *Minolta XG-M with 400mm lens; f5.6 at 1/250 sec; Ektachrome 100*

HIGHLY COMMENDED

BELA BERTA (HUNGARY)
GREAT CRESTED GREBE

"Having found a pond with great crested grebes that weren't shy, I thought it would be easy to photograph them. But either it was windy or the water was rough or it was rainy or the birds were not active – it took 35 days to get this picture."

● *Canon AL1 with 400mm lens; monopod; f8 at 1/250 sec; Kodachrome 64*

HIGHLY COMMENDED

JEFF VANUGA (USA)
ANHINGA (right)

"The anhinga feeds on fish, which it catches as it swims through the water. After hunting, the bird perches on a branch and suns itself. Because the anhinga has no natural oils on its feathers, it must dry its wings before flying. What caught my attention on this occasion were the highlights on the bird."

● *Nikon F4 with 500mm lens; tripod; Fujichrome 50*

HANS CHRISTOPH KAPPEL
(GERMANY)
SPOONBILL

"Thrusting its head forward, the spoonbill swallows a fish after first tossing it in the air to catch it in the right position. I took the picture from my car beside Lake Neusiedl in Austria just to finish off a film and it was two months before I saw the results."

● *Canon F1 with 800mm lens; f5.6; Ektachrome 64*

7

HIGHLY COMMENDED

PAUL TAYLOR (UK)

CAPERCAILLIE DISPLAYING

''The courtship display of the capercaillie is one of the wildlife highlights of the Highland year. Photographing it is not difficult once the lek has been found, but I had to be in the hide by three o'clock every morning to be ready for the display, which begins around dawn.''

● *Nikon FE2 with 300mm lens; tripod; f2.8 at 1/30 sec; Kodachrome 64*

HIGHLY COMMENDED

PETER BÁRDOS DEÁK (HUNGARY)

BEARDED TITS (left)

''Bearded tits always roost in groups — they jostle one another to get closer together as if terrified of being alone. After they've all taken their place, the one at the end will stretch its neck and then jump onto the back of the others, pushing its way in with its feet. This jostling for positions goes on until they all fall asleep — the moment captured in the picture.''

● *Minolta MD; flash; f11; Ektachrome 64*

JEAN FRANÇOIS HELLIO (FRANCE)
& NICOLAS VAN INGEN (HOLLAND)
AVOCET DEFENDING NEST

"The avocet had made its nest on a patch used by cows. Here it is bravely trying to defend its eggs, even touching the nose of the cow with its bill. The picture was taken in the Marais Breton in Vendée, France. We were doing a study on avocets."

● *Nikon FE2 with 400mm lens; tripod; f5.6 at 1/250 sec; Kodachrome 64*

HANS CHRISTOPH KAPPEL
(GERMANY)

HUMMINGBIRD HAWKMOTH

"Although it is a hawkmoth, this species is active during the day. It feeds on nectar, hovering over the flower and probing it with its long proboscis. I took the image as part of a series on flying insects. Hummingbird hawkmoths move about very quickly, and so I put drops of honey juice into the calyx of a flower to attract one. Another problem is the speed at which the wings are moving — to catch them on film, a number of flashes are needed. In this case four on the hawkmoth and flower, and four for the background.''

● *Canon T90 with 400mm lens; flashlights; f11 at 1/60 sec; Kodachrome 64*

8

YURI SHIBNEV (USSR)
MOTH EMERGING

Yuri Shibnev works as an ornithologist at the Kedrovapad Reserve close to the border with China, an area that was completely closed to foreigners until very recently. Despite lack of modern camera equipment and funds to buy film, he tries to photograph as much of the wildlife on the reserve as possible. Much of his effort is devoted to catching the rare Amur leopard on film. As part of this project, Yuri has been photographing cocoons and the insects that emerge from them; the moth in this picture is *Rhodinia fugax diana*. Yuri heard about the competition from a BBC producer who visited the reserve while filming for a series, *Realms of the Russian Bear*, to be broadcast in 1992.

● *Pentacon 6TL with 80mm lens; Ektachrome 64*

UWE ANDERS (GERMANY)
MARSHLAND DARTERS

"These marshland darters have spent the night among vegetation. In the early morning, each male attaches himself to a female, to mate, he has a mate when the females go down to the water to lay their eggs around midday. The picture was taken in the Camargue, southern France, while I was studying dragonflies."

● *Canon T-90 with 200mm lens; f5.6 at 1/750 sec; Kodachrome 64*

SCOTT CAMAZINE (USA)
HONEY BEES

"I do research on honeybees, and took this picture of a mass of bees clustering compactly on their comb in Bangalore, India."

● *Nikon 8008 with 55mm lens; flash; f16; Kodachrome 64*

LUIZ CLAUDIO MARIGO (BRAZIL)
HAMADRYAS BUTTERFLY (right)

"This photo was taken in the Amazon forest in Serra dos Carajas during the month of May. The 'click' butterfly Hamadryas februa rests upside down on tree trunks where it is well camouflaged."

● *200mm lens; flash and reflectors*

MARK MATTOCK (UK)
HONEYBEE NEST IN A WOODPECKER HOLE

"This is one of the images taken for a book project about the wildlife of my garden. It was not actually taken in the garden, but is important because it shows where the hundreds of bees constantly in the garden come from. The hole was lit with two flash heads to show the bees on the rim and to pick out the cells at the back. I received over 30 stings, and retreated in agony after completing a roll of film."

• *Nikon F4s with 105 macro lens; Kodachrome 25*

MIKE GILLAM (AUSTRALIA)
HONEY POT ANTS

"In order to study the feasibility of maintaining a living display of honey pot ants, we built an artificial nest with underground chambers connected to a surface habitat for foraging worker ants. In this picture you can see a worker ant with the 'replexes' ants hanging from the roof of the chamber, their abdomens full of 'honey'. The ants act as living storage chambers to provide food for the colony during the extended dry season. Located up to one metre underground, these storage chambers remain cool and humid in stark contrast to the high temperatures above ground in the central Australian desert regions."

• *Canon F1 with 105mm lens; flash; f16; Kodachrome 25*

CHRIS KNIGHTS (UK)
DRAGONFLY

"While I was using a hide to photograph snipe at Westcare I watched dragonflies hover once or twice over a particular spot, and so I decided to focus on them and take a few shots." Chris Knights combines life as a farmer in East Anglia with wildlife photography. He has also done film work for Survival Anglia.

● *Canon EOS620 with 300mm lens; tripod; f8 at 1/350 sec; Kodachrome 200*

ERLING SCHÖN (SWEDEN)
SNAIL

"I wanted to take a good photo of a small animal that everyone can enjoy, if they just take the time to stop and bend down for a minute. This snail, *Cepaea hortensis*, is common throughout Sweden so I just had to wait for the right moment – a warm wet day with soft sunlight when the snails would be very active."

● *Nikon 801 with 105mm lens; f8 at 1/30 sec; Fujichrome Velviu 50*

RUNNER-UP

GABRIELE SOMENZI (ITALY)
JUMPING SPIDER

''I had seen this scene, of a jumping spider pouncing on a fly, many times before, and I took it as a challenge to capture the crucial moment of action on film.'' Gabriele Somenzi specializes in macrophotography of insects in flight.

● *Nikon FE2 with micro lens; flash; f11; Kodachrome 25*

WINNER

Pam Kemp (UK)

SHARK WITH NET MARKS

"The shark, a short-nosed black-tail, was one of a number of juveniles taken from a fisherman's net in the Seychelles. We spotted them as the nets were being pulled in, and as soon as we were able, we took this one back into the sea. Sadly it had been too damaged and did not survive. Juveniles of this species often die like this — what a tragic waste."

● *Nikonos V with 15mm lens; flash; f5.6; Fujichrome 50*

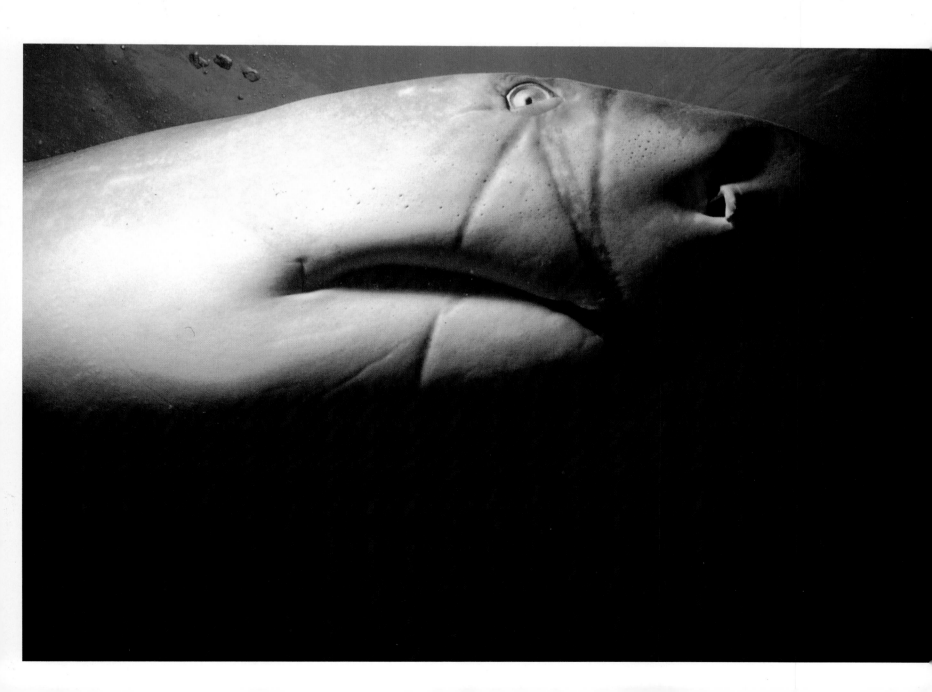

VINCENT McGOLDRICK (UK)
HUMANS CAN SERIOUSLY DAMAGE YOUR HEALTH

"The chimp put its hand out, like a child asking for a sweet, and someone threw him a packet of cigarettes and a box of matches. Mimicking members of the public who were smoking, it proceeded to light up and smoke. The chimp was in an enclosure in the Safari Park at Derwock, Northern Ireland."

● *Yashica 230 with 70-210mm lens; f5.6 at 1/250 sec; Fujichrome 100*

CHRIS GILLMAN (UK)
CAPTIVE CHIMPANZEE (right)

"The chimpanzee was frantic and I wanted to give some impression of his torment. Eventually he stayed still enough to permit this shot. The zoo – Patan Zoo, Nepal – is typical of those in the Third World. The conditions endured by the animals are very cramped and dirty."

● *Canon T90 with 70-210mm lens; Fujichrome 100*

HIGHLY COMMENDED

KENNAN WARD (USA)
BALD EAGLE VICTIM (left)

"Bald eagles congregate at Kachemak Bay in Alaska to feed on salmon returning from the sea to spawn. This bird must have picked up a discarded remnant of halibut with the hook still in – unfortunately, the fishermen keep them very sharp. It was still able to feed and didn't seem particularly distressed, but this image certainly gets across the message that fishermen, like everyone else, should take more care with their waste."

● *Nikon F4 with 500mm lens; Kodachrome 64*

HIGHLY COMMENDED

NATALINO FENECH (MALTA)
IN THE NAME OF GAME

"The picture was taken in Dingly, Malta, and shows song thrushes, fieldfares and a skylark, all of which are considered gamebirds and are shot for fun. They were found wrapped in newspaper, and I don't know whether they were thrown away or fell from the hunter's bag. I took the picture to show people what goes on while they are still asleep – most hunting on Malta takes place away from the public eye."

● *Nikon FE2 with 50mm lens; Kodachrome 64*

HIGHLY COMMENDED

MORLEY READ (UK)
OPOSSUM

"This baby opossum was found half-drowned in water trapped around a well head in the Ecuadorian Amazon. We rescued it but before running away it faced the camera and squealed. I visited the site, a British Gas exploratory well, while undertaking research for Friends of the Earth UK on the environmental problems created by oil drilling."

● *Pentax 645 with 45mm lens; Fujichrome 100*

HIGHLY COMMENDED

ROGER GRACE (NEW ZEALAND)
PACIFIC WHITE-SIDED DOLPHIN DROWNED IN DRIFTNET

"I was taking photographs on a Greenpeace expedition to the North Pacific to document marine life killed in oceanic driftnets. This fishing technique is extremely wasteful, catching and killing large numbers of fish, birds, mammals and turtles as an accidental by-catch. In this instance, the fishermen were targeting squid, but killed many other species including this Pacific white-sided dolphin."

● *Nikonos V with 15mm lens; strobes; f8 at 1/60 sec; Fujichrome 50*

RICHARD PACKWOOD (UK)
DEAD FOREST

"I had never before seen the effects of severe acid rain pollution, and was not prepared for the total devastation of dead and broken trees. At first I was convinced that I was looking at the results of a forest fire. I took the picture in the notorious pollution triangle where Germany, Poland and Czechoslovakia meet. At the time I was on a seven-month photographic trip to Eastern Europe."

● *Nikon FM2 with 20mm lens; f8 at 1/60 sec; Koda-chrome 64*

COLIN PRIOR (UK)
DEFORESTATION (below)
"I was in Ilheus in the state of Bahia, Brazil, to photograph
the habitat of the rare golden-headed lion tamarin. The
animal is now extremely endangered because of forest loss.

● *Linhof Technorama 6175; f22 at 1 sec; Fujichrome Velvia*

MARTIN WENDLER (GERMANY)
ILLEGAL TRADE

"I have been documenting the illegal trade in wild animals and also the so-called 'legal' hunting and trade that goes on within the CITES agreement. As part of this project, I photographed this pile of skins in Munich airport. The skins which include leopard and cheetah from Africa and puma from the USA, had been confiscated by Customs officials."

● *Canon EOSI; flash; Fujichrome 50*

WINNER

ANDRÉ BÄRTSCHI (LIECHTENSTEIN)
JAGUAR

"I have been returning to Manu National Park in south-eastern Peru for many years now. I had my first encounter with a jaguar back in 1978 but I've never before managed such a close photograph. One morning as I was walking back to camp, I noticed something large moving through the forest understorey – a jaguar was clambering onto a fallen trunk where it lay down with its back towards me. I moved closer and set up my tripod. It never did seem to notice me, probably because the damp leaf litter muffled my footsteps."

● *Nikon F4 with 400mm lens; tripod; f3.5 at 1/30 sec; Kodachrome 64*

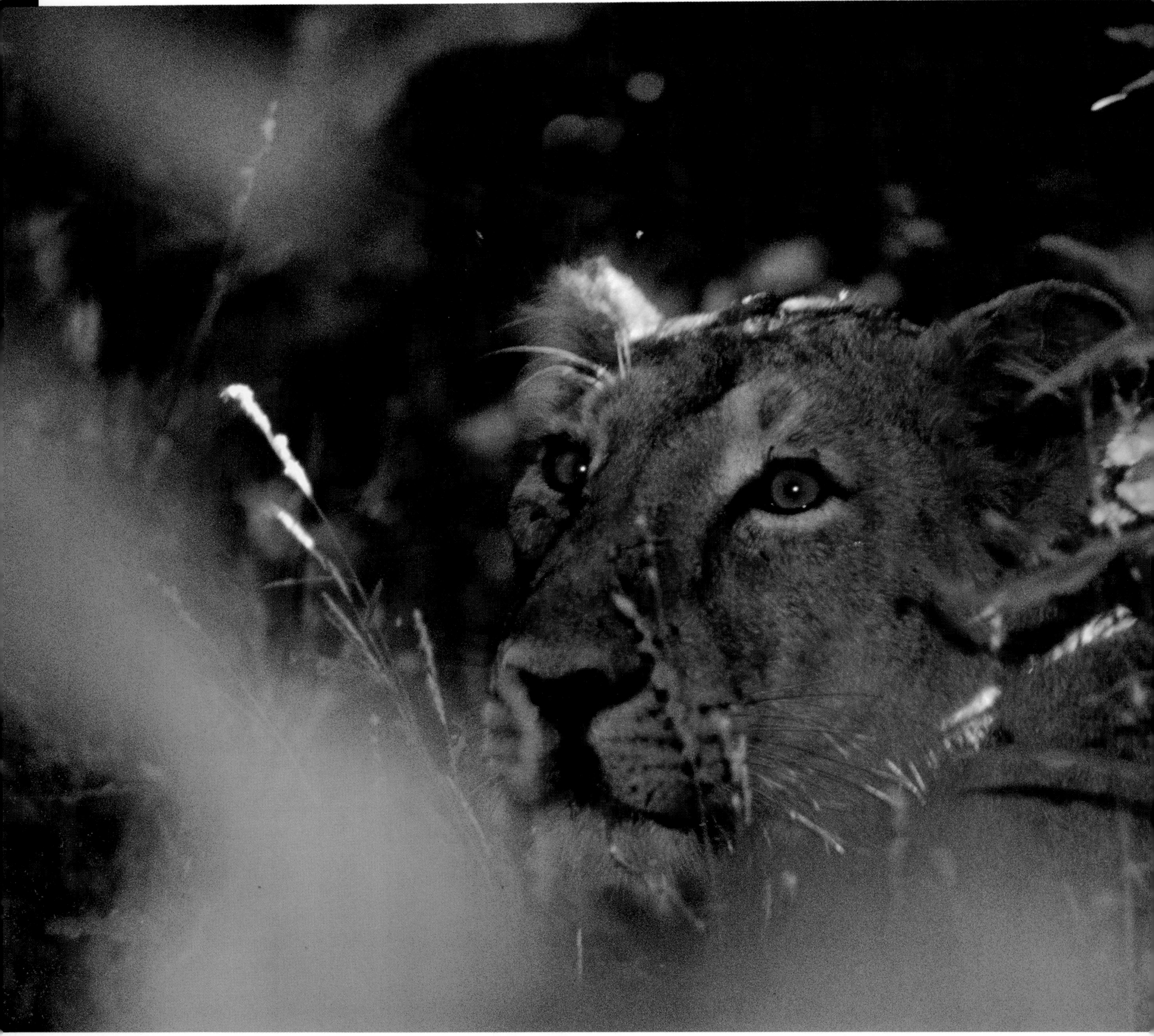

ANTTI LEINONEN (FINLAND)

WOLVERINE

"The wolverine is the most endangered large animal in Finland – there are only about 40 individuals living in the forests near the eastern border. I have worked in the area for several years from a hide, putting out carrion mainly to encourage the bears but sometimes, as on this occasion in July, wolverines are also attracted."

- *Canon A1 with 560mm lens; Fuji RHP 400*

RUNNER·UP

SUNJOY MONGA (INDIA)

ASIATIC LION (left)

"I was waiting in dense, humid undergrowth in the Gir forest, in western India, when I spotted this lion just eight feet away. It was October just after the monsoon when the luxuriant vegetation makes it difficult to see the lions – of which there are only a few hundred left, all in this forest. I was making a film about them, so wanted to get some footage at all times of the year."

- *Nikon FE with 200mm lens; flash; f4; Fujichrome 100*

ERWIN & PEGGY BAUER (USA)

GREY WOLF

"I photographed this grey wolf during a very cold February day in the valley of the North Fork of the Flathead River, Montana. During the past few years, grey wolves have been moving southward from British Columbia and Alberta to recolonise the state. I first saw a wild wolf there in 1989. Seeing the return of a native has been among the greatest thrills I have experienced."

● *Nikon F4 with 300mm lens; 1/500 sec; Kodachrome 200*

DAVE ROBINSON (UK)

TIGER

"All my holidays are spent photographing wildlife in wild places. I took this shot in Ranthambhore National Park, India. It was evening when we saw this tigress weaving her way through tall grasses towards a small herd of sambar and chital grazing in the lake. She disappeared and after about 45 minutes I spotted her moving in the undergrowth. She made a silent kill and came out dragging a young chital. I took this photo as she paused cautiously on her way back into the forest, where we knew she had three cubs waiting."

● *Canon T90 with 300mm lens; f2.8 at 1/125 sec; Kodachrome 64*

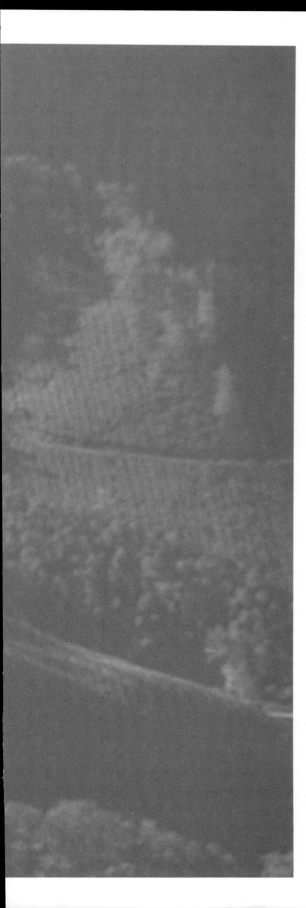

HIGHLY COMMENDED

KENNAN WARD (USA)

HUMPBACK WHALE BREACHING

"I was watching a group of humpback whales feeding together in south-east Alaska; as the group split up and went in different directions, all the humpbacks started breaching."

● *Nikon F3 with 80-200mm lens; Kodachrome 64*

HIGHLY COMMENDED

A K RAJU (INDIA)

NILIGIRI TAHR (left)

"Four days of patience and mountaineering produced this picture of niligiri tahr standing on a high cliff overlooking a tea estate in Ervikulam Wildlife Sanctuary, Kerala, India. When last counted, the numbers of this animal were estimated at about 2,000, though this may now be increasing because of protection."

● *Nikon FM2 with 80-200mm lens; f8 at 1/60 sec; Fujichrome 100*

FRANCISCO MÁRQUEZ (SPAIN)
LAMMERGEIER

"The lammergeier is one of the most interesting birds in Spain but it is also one of the rarest and most difficult to photograph. To get this picture I went high in the Pyrenees mountains and constructed a well-camouflaged hide where I spent 15 hours a day over a three-week period. I put out the carcass of a dead sheep and then waited, hoping that lammergeier would appear. Griffon vultures came first and then two days later, when only the bones were left, lammergeier started to make brief visits."

● *Nikon F4s with 500mm lens; tripod; Fujichrome Velvia 50*

Frans Lanting
(THE NETHERLANDS)
LILY PADS

"This is the Okavango from below – it's a different world down there. I was sitting on the bottom of the river when I took the shot. I would plunge in, hold my breath for a minute, try to shoot, and then come up for air and go down again. Because there can be a crocodile around the bend, it shouldn't be done in any one spot for long and I try to choose a position where there isn't too much underwater vegetation – it's a calculated risk."

• *Nikon FE with wide-angle lens in an underwater housing*

JAN TÖVE JOHANSSON (SWEDEN)
BIRCH TREES

"Birch is a very common tree in Sweden. Towards the north of the country the trunks become whiter as the air is cleaner. The picture was taken one late afternoon close to a lake east of Gothenburg. The light was special and I was attracted by the background colours. Seeing all the trunks together gave me the idea for the composition."

● *Pentax 645 with 600mm lens; f5.6 at 1/60; Ektachrome 64*

PAUL TAYLOR (UK)
BIRCH AND HEATHERS (left)

"I stopped off at Morrone Birkwood in Deeside on my way home from a day's walking in the Cairngorms. The wood is one of the finest upland birchwoods in Britain, similar to those in Norway. The weather was miserable but the low light and rain created almost abstract compositions with the green foliage of the birches and soft purple of the heather. On this occasion I found exactly what I wanted – a single old birch at the base of a heatherbank."

● *Nikon FE2 with 105mm lens; tripod; f16/22 at 1/2 sec; Kodachrome 64*

HIGHLY COMMENDED

DANIEL J COX (USA)

FIREWEED

"Fireweed is one of the first flowers to grow after a fire. I took this picture in Yellowstone National Park two years after the fires that swept through the area in 1988."

● *Nikon F3 with 300mm lens; Kodachrome 64*

DAVID NOTON (UK)

LLYN BARFOG

''I was on an early morning ramble with my wife, looking for vantage points for classic Welsh landscape shots, when we found these water lilies in this remote and peaceful lake.''

● *Olympus OM1n with 21mm lens and polariser; f5.6; Fujichrome 50*

HIGHLY COMMENDED

GEORGE S K CHIEW (MALAYSIA)
RAFFLESIA (left)

"Rafflesia is a very rare parasitic plant, which no nature lover would miss the chance of seeing or photographing. This one was found in primary jungle twenty miles from Kuching, an area that is currently being logged. The three-foot wide flower had just bloomed, and the petals were firm to the touch. Although one or two flies were around, the flower had not yet started to develop the characteristic rotten smell."

● *Nikon F801 with 55mm macro lens; tripod; flash; Fujichrome 100*

HIGHLY COMMENDED

ALLAN G POTTS (UK)
FLY AGARIC

"As I was driving away from Harbottle woods my attention was drawn to a meadow grazed by sheep and surrounded by a high stone wall. To my delight I found the biggest group of fly agaric I have ever seen, 20 perfect specimens, the largest measuring 24 centimetres. Needless to say I spent some two hours exposing three rolls of film – a memorable moment that only nature can offer."

● *Nikon F4 with 24mm lens; tripod; f11 at 1/15 sec; Fujichrome Velvia 50*

HIGHLY COMMENDED

JORMA PEIPONEN (FINLAND)
DAISY, DEW AND SPIDER (right)

"I had been photographing the hunting behaviour of spiders, and found this one on an ox-eye daisy very early one summer morning. It is waiting for an insect, such as a butterfly, to visit the flower."

● *Nikon F3 with 200mm macro lens; tripod; f16 at 4 sec; Kodachrome 64*

HIGHLY COMMENDED

STEVEN FULLER (USA)
FROSTED TREE

"This lodgepole pine grows on a rimrock cliff overlooking a thermal area in Yellowstone Park. It is January shortly after sunrise and the temperature is about 45°F below zero. Down below, a steam vent fumerole pumps moisture into the air. This freezes into hexagonal plates of frost crystals which are lofted upward to tumble and drift in the cold clear air. Each plate acts like a mirror and reflects the brilliant morning light from the sun, which has just crested the horizon directly behind the tree."

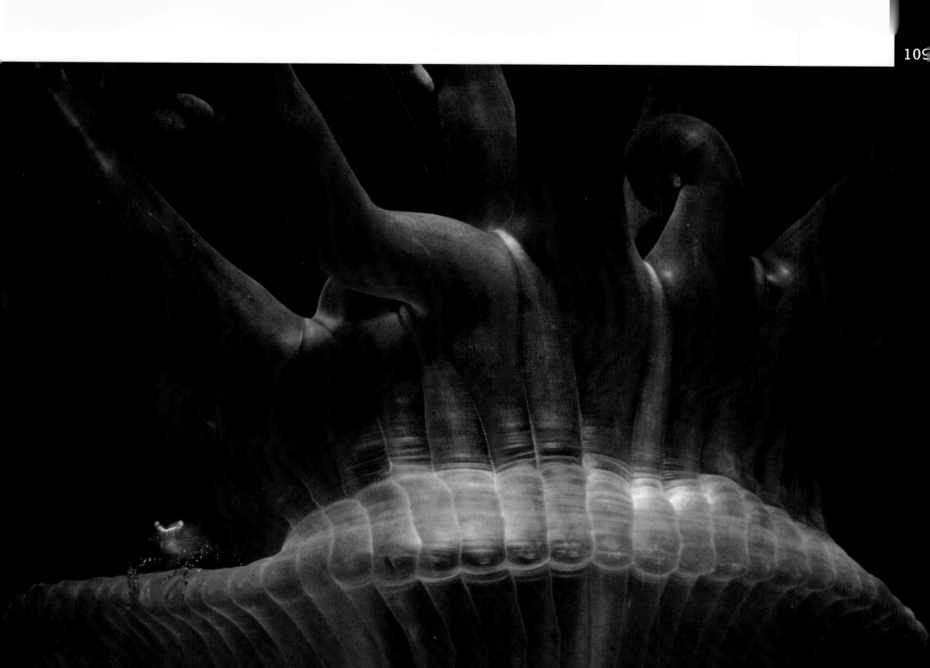

JEFFREY L ROTMAN (USA)
SHRIMP AND ANEMONE

"On a dive in the Red Sea off the Sinai peninsula, I stopped to inspect an anemone and found a shrimp living with it. The anemone and shrimp live in a symbiotic relationship – the shrimp keeps the anemone clean and in return is protected from predators by the anemone's tentacles. I am a professional underwater photographer and try to focus my work on the inter-relationships between animals in their environment."

● *Nikonos II with 28mm lens and 2:1 extension tube; flash and reflector; f22; Kodachrome 64*

ALLEN WAYNE CAMPBELL (USA)

GOBY ON RED CORAL

"Soft corals are abundant in the Red Sea and come in all colours. It is a real treat when you find the creatures that make their home in them. This goby fish is just 3.5 centimetres long and lives amongst the coral's 'stalks' for protection. I managed just two shots before it vanished. The picture was taken on a night dive off the coast of Egypt."

● *Nikon F3 with 55mm lens; underwater housing; substrobes; f16 at 1/60 sec; Fujichrome Velvia 50*

ANDY BELCHER (NEW ZEALAND)
RED SEA URCHIN

"We had a noisy group of divers on the boat off Poor Knights Island and I couldn't sleep, so we decided to go for a night dive. I found the red sea urchin *Diadema palmeri* on a sandy bottom and decided to photograph it against a background of kelp."

● *Nikonos V with 28mm lens; strobes; f22 at 1/90 sec; Kodachrome 64*

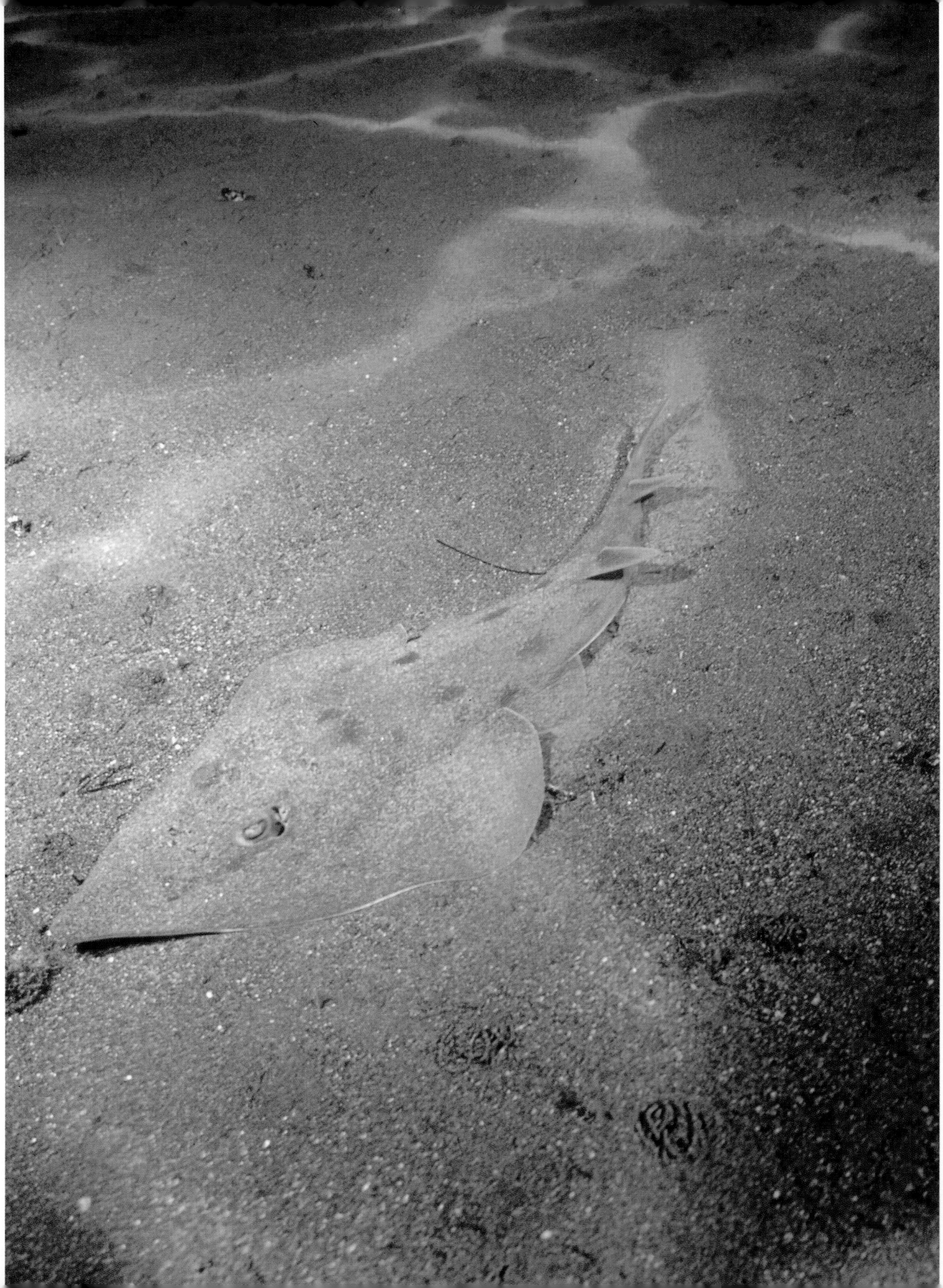

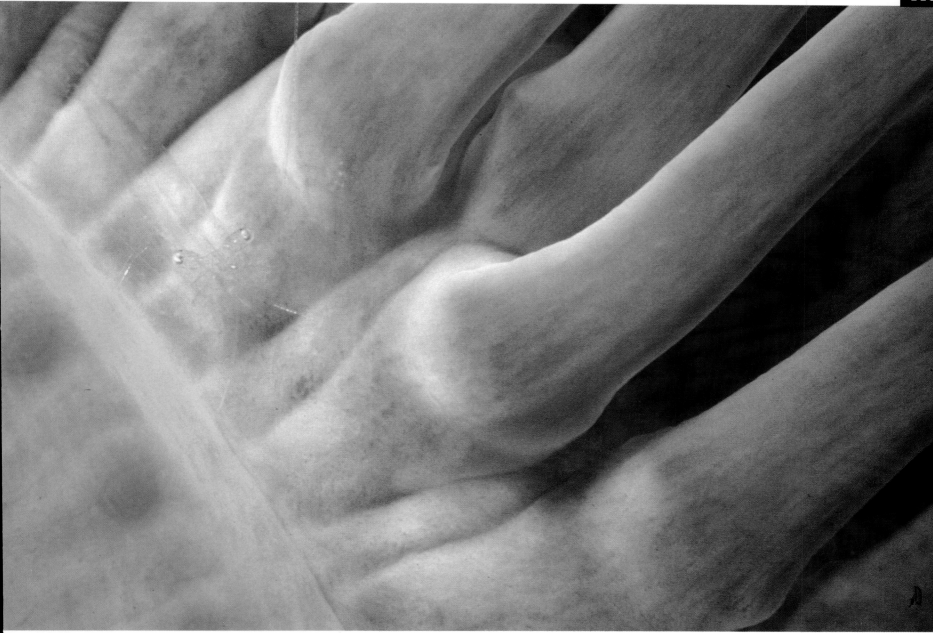

RICHARD HERRMANN (USA)

GUITARFISH (left)

"When the sun is out, you often get this interesting dappling effect on sandy bottoms in shallow water. It is not so hard to capture with available light but is difficult to blend with strobe light. In this case, luck and taking a number of shots led to a successful image. The shot was taken near Catalina Island, off the Californian coast."

● *Nikonos V with 20mm lens; strobes; f8 at 1/90 sec; Fujichrome Velvia pushed to 100ISO*

LINDA PITKIN (UK)

TRANSPARENT SHRIMP AND ANEMONE

"Shrimps often live in association with anemones in the tropics, but they can be difficult to spot as they are tiny as well as being well camouflaged."

● *Nikonos V with 35mm lens and 1:1 extension tubes; f16-22 at 1/60 sec; flash; Kodachrome 64*

LINDA PITKIN (UK)
SILVERSIDES

"The shoal of tiny fish came in close to the boat we were staying on off the Maldive Islands. They were so tightly packed together that, from the surface, their shadow looked like a submerged rock, except that it moved. The photograph was taken in a shallow sandy lagoon and the fish are lit by a combination of sunlight and flash."

● *Nikonos V with 15mm lens; flash with diffuser; f8-11 at 1/60 sec; Kodachrome 64*

DARRYL TORCKLER (NEW ZEALAND)
GANNET COLONY (right)

"High up on a cliff platform at Murawai is one of New Zealand's two mainland colonies of Australasian gannets. Since 1986, I have been trying to take a moonlit-gannet-colony shot to enter in this competition. On this occasion, I arrived just before sunset; the sky was clear and the moon nearly full. I started taking pictures but then the clouds came scudding over, intermittently blocking out the moon. I got one more shot in the fast fading light, with moonlight for half the exposure time. When I closed the shutter it was pitch black, cold and starting to rain."

● *Canon F1 with 35-105mm lens; blue filter; tripod; double exposure, main picture; f4 at 8 mins; moon: 300mm lens and f5.6 at 1/250 sec; Fujichrome Velvia 50*

MIKE OSMOND (AUSTRALIA)
HUMPBACK WHALES

"I am involved in research on humpback whales and was following these animals in Hervey Bay, Queensland, to record details of their flukes for identification purposes." Mike Osmond works as a marine park ranger and photographs all aspects of marine life.

● *Canon T90 with 85mm lens; Kodachrome 200*

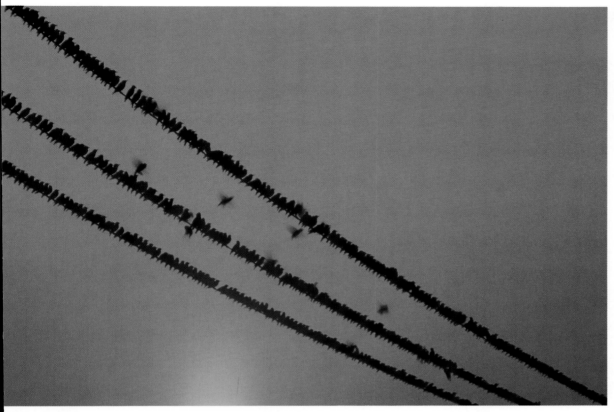

TERRY NEWMAN (UK)

STARLINGS

"I was driving home at dusk without my camera when I saw starlings gathering to roost in nearby reedbeds. I thought they might make an exciting shot, and decided to return the following evening. I took several shots before and after the sun had set."

● *Nikkormat EL with 135mm lens; Kodachrome 64*

JEREMY OWEN (UK)

EMPEROR PENGUINS

"The emperor penguins were gathered on Brunt ice shelf in Antarctica to breed. It was about 30 degrees Centigrade below freezing, and in these conditions film frequently breaks."

● *Olympus OM2n with 28-85mm lens; f5.6 at 1/30 sec*

JOHN & KAREN HOLLINGSWORTH (USA)

MOOSE AMONGST CATTAILS

"We were photographing nesting waterfowl in the wetlands of Seedskadee National Wildlife Refuge, Wyoming, and at sunset decided to concentrate on last year's cattails backlit by a fiery glow. As we were taking pictures, a cow moose stood up and we included her in the photograph. We found out later that she had just given birth."

● *Nikon F4 with 500mm lens; window mount; f5.6 at 1/500 sec; Fujichrome 100*

NICK GARBUTT (UK)

MAURITIUS KESTRELS (right)

"The conservation of the Mauritius kestrel is an undoubted success. Like its European cousin, it is also proving adaptable to urban environments. I was the foster parent to this pair which were released near St Louis, the capital of the island. When the photograph was taken they were two months old and still learning hunting skills. The bird on the left was watching a fallen leaf; the other was probably asleep."

● *Nikon FE2 with 300mm lens; tripod; f5.6 at 1/500 sec; Fujichrome Velvia 50*

MARK MATTOCK (UK)
FROG AMONGST MILK BOTTLES

"The frog is one of many that live in my garden and breed in the pond. In the evening they can be found in various sites around the garden. Despite its man-made setting, the frog is very well camouflaged amongst the milk bottles."

● *Nikon F4s with 55mm lens; flash; Kodachrome 25*

MARK MATTOCK (UK)
SUBURBAN SERENGETI

"This photo of garlic mustard plants is one of the environmental or landscape images for a book that I am currently working on entitled *Suburban Serengeti*. The idea is to show the garden as a truly wild place from the point of view of the creatures that live in it, just as wild as any forest in the world but on a much smaller scale. To find this particular scene, I followed the local hedgehog's regular route and adopted his viewpoint."

● *Nikon F4s with 24mm lens; Kodachrome 25*

MARTIN D LILLICRAP (UK)
BRAMBLE

"I took this picture because the fresh bright green leaves against the dark wood of a dilapidated wooden shed was very striking. The symbolism of the image – new growth amidst decay – only struck me afterwards. I used a bit of Blu-tak to keep the leaves still in the strong breeze."

● *Minolta X700 with 90mm lens; f22; Fujichrome 50*

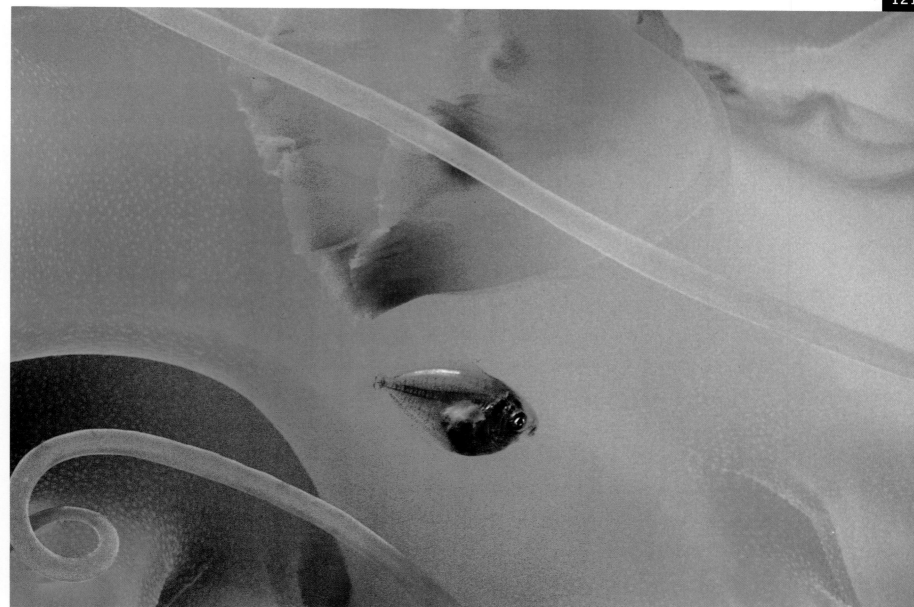

RICHARD HERRMANN (USA)
COMMENSAL FISH AND JELLYFISH

''Juvenile Pacific butterfish are often found with the jellyfish, *Pelagia colorata*, a rather large jellyfish whose bell can be a metre wide. Apparently, the jellyfish gains nothing from this association although the fish receives protection from the jellyfish's stinging tentacles. The picture was taken five miles off the coast of California where 90 per cent of my photographs are taken. I specialise in marine subjects, above water as well as below.''

● *Nikon F with 55mm micro lens; underwater housing; strobe; f16 at 1/60 sec*

STEVEN FULLER (USA)
SNOW STUDY
"Yellowstone National Park, February 1990, two years after the great fires. Burnt snags of trees cast shadows that trace the contours of the snow-covered hills creating a juxta-position of vertical and horizontal patterns." Steven Fuller lives in Yellowstone.

● *Nikon with 80-200mm lens; Kodachrome 64*

PAULI NIEMINEN (FINLAND)

BIRCH TREES

"The forest holds many possibilities for a photographer. The white trunks and fresh green spring leaves were the inspiration for this image. Light, colour and rhythm are the essential elements."

● *Canon EOS with 80-200mm lens; tripod; f16 at 1/30 sec; Fujichrome 100*

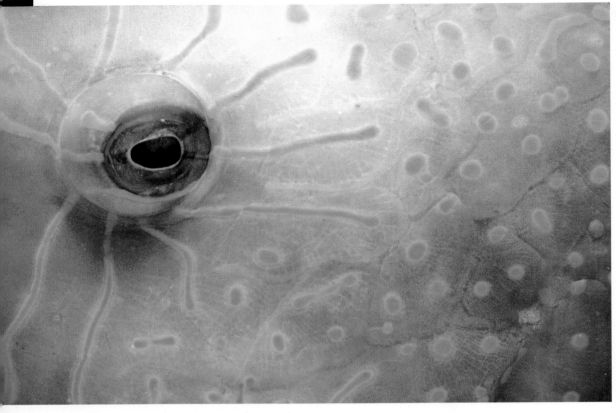

JEFFREY L ROTMAN (USA)
EYE OF WRASSE

"The lines surrounding the wrasse's eye are meant to confuse a predator, which will aim for this spot on the fish. At the time, I was working on a story about the different types of eye that fish have. The picture was taken in the Red Sea off the Sinai peninsula."

● *Nikonos II with 28mm lens and extension tube; flash; f22; Kodachrome 64*

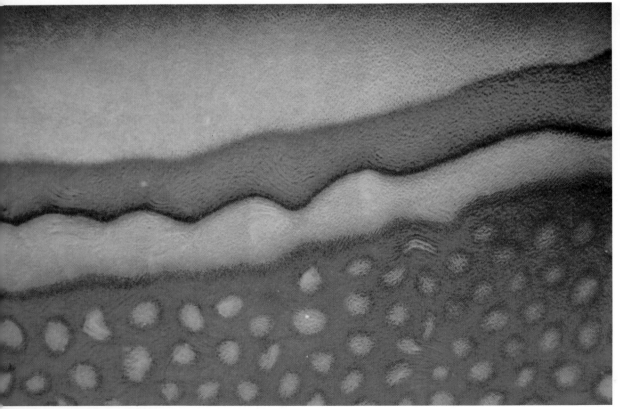

JEFFREY L ROTMAN (USA)
PARROTFISH SKIN

"This picture was taken in the Red Sea off Ras Nas Rani in the Sinai peninsula, Egypt. It was night and the parrotfish was asleep in a coral cave 70 feet down. At the time, I was working on a story for *Smithsonian* magazine about fish skin colours and textures and their role in communication."

● *Nikonos II with 28mm lens and 3:1 extension tube; flash; f22; Kodachrome 64*

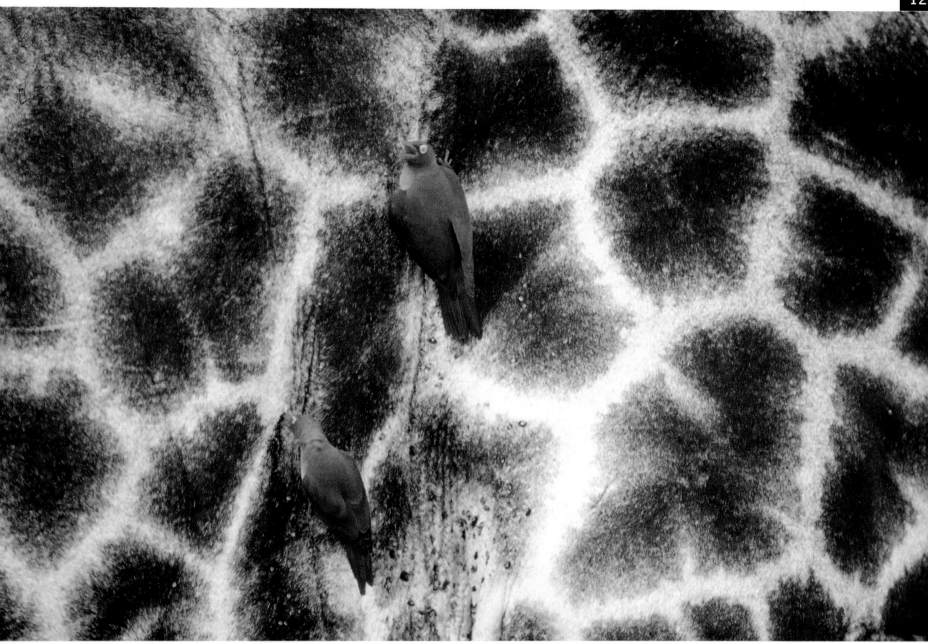

LEX HES (SOUTH AFRICA)
OXPECKERS

"These are red-billed oxpeckers feeding on the parasites to be found on a giraffe. The animal let me approach close enough to fill the frame with its skin."

● *Nikon FM2 with 300mm lens; Kodachrome 64*

BOBBY TULLOCH (UK)

GANNETS

''I was giving a commentary from the bridge on the National Trust for Scotland's annual cruise when a flock of gannets gathered over the wake of the ship. I handed the microphone to someone else and grabbed my camera.''

● *Pentax with 28-70mm lens; Afga 100*

KIM WESTERSKOV (NEW ZEALAND)

SEASCAPE AND ALBATROSS (right)

''South West Cape was exhilarating, if not terrifying, with huge waves crashing against the cliffs and outlying rocks. White-capped and light-mantled sooty albatrosses soared effortlessly in front of the maelstrom. I was in a small dive-charter vessel in the Auckland Islands skippered by an adventurous New Zealander who took us much closer to the cliffs than normal!''

● *Canon FIN with 80-200mm lens; 1/500 sec; Kodachrome 64*

DAVID NOTON (UK)
OLD MAN OF STORR

"The shot was taken during a two-week shoot in Scotland. I was camped on the Isle of Skye near the Old Man of Storr, looking for a different viewpoint of this famous feature. Most people photograph it from down below but I decided to climb up to some cliffs overlooking it. The light was good and the visibility superb — you could see all the way to the mainland. Typically for Scotland, the shot was taken between rain showers."

● *Olympus OM1n with 28mm lens; polarizing and graduated filters; f5.6 at 1/60 sec; Fujichrome 50*

JOHN WARDEN (USA)

AURORA BOREALIS

"I go to Alaska's Denali Park every September, because that's when the wildlife is in its prime. As the arctic night sets in and the weather gets colder, it's also a good time for auroras. An aurora is the ultimate light show for a photographer — it's like the skies are dancing above you and the whole of space seems to be moving around. You have to be a bit lucky when you open the shutter, but I've come to know through experience how long to give the exposure."

● *Nikon F3 with 28mm lens; f2.8 at 30 secs; Fujichrome 100 pushed one stop*

BOYD NORTON (USA)
AUGUSTINE VOLCANO

"I was in Kamishak Bay, Alaska, to photograph bears when I had the opportunity to get this shot of Augustine volcano, which had erupted three months previously. Most days were foggy or rainy but on this occasion it was clear enough to show the volcano, steam pouring from its vent, against beautiful dawn colours."

● *Leica R4 with 70-210mm zoom lens; tripod; Kodachrome 64*

FRANS LANTING
(THE NETHERLANDS)
HIPPOPOTAMUS

"I was at the edge of the water and close enough to the hippo for there to be tension in the air. He was obviously telling me that he didn't want me there. He is showing off how big and mean he is with the kind of bluff behaviour that I have seen over the years in animals from elephant seals to lizards. Most animals prefer to displace you without actually having to attack. I think the picture succeeds because it shows a rather different view of hippos. In Okavango they are a force to be reckoned with and kill more people than any other big mammal. They have no qualms about biting a person in half — look at his tusks!"

● *Nikon FE with telephoto lens*

RUNNER-UP

RICH KIRCHNER (USA)
RED KANGAROO

"I had been trying to get good photos of red kangaroos for some time but the kangaroos and the light simply were not cooperating. Finally, early one morning, I found this lone kangaroo feeding in the open. The sun rose above the ridge behind me and illuminated the scene putting the sparkle in his eyes."

● *Nikon F4 with 500mm lens; tripod; f5.6 at 1/250 sec; Kodachrome 64*

HIGHLY COMMENDED

CLAUDE STEELMAN (USA)
PRONGHORN

"I had seen antelope drinking at a particular waterhole so I constructed a hide near it. About two weeks later I entered the hide before daylight and waited three hours for the antelope to come to drink. The changing aspen trees created a colourful background, which is unusual for antelope habitat. The picture was taken in north-western Colorado."

● *Nikon FE2 with 300mm lens; tripod; f8 at 1/125 sec; Kodachrome 64*

BEN OSBORNE (UK)

TIMBER WOLF

"As a professional photographer I have worked in extreme environments, in Antarctica and in high mountains. But I'm not averse to taking the easy option now and again — hence this picture taken in a wildlife park in Scotland. The wolves were in a large enclosure and the heavy chain-link fence made photography difficult. But a slow shutter speed with the lens at full aperture threw the wire out of focus, rendering it practically invisible."

● *Nikon F4s with 300mm lens and x4 converter*

MONIKA DUSCHER (AUSTRIA)
LIONESS

"The secret behind the spotlight effect in the picture is snow. The photograph was taken on a particularly sunny February day in London Zoo. The lioness was indoors, near a window and the snow acted as a giant reflector. When somebody walked by attracting the animal's attention I took the picture."

● *Nikon with 80-200mm lens; Fujichrome Velvia 50*

HIGHLY COMMENDED

RICH KIRCHNER (USA)

DALL RAM

"The picture was taken in Denali National Park, Alaska. I spent the better part of the day climbing up a ridge to a group of dall sheep. This impressive ram was just lying there chewing the cud, sleeping and looking over his domain. I was lucky enough to have all the necessary elements come together when he decided to lip-curl. 'Lip-curl' display is normally associated with the rutting season and usually occurs after the ram sniffs urine – either of a ewe, or another ram or, as in this case, their own."

● *Nikon FA with 300mm lens; tripod; f5.6 at 1/500 sec; Fujichrome 100 Professional*

HIGHLY COMMENDED

WILLIAM S PATON (UK)

AFRICAN BUFFALO (left)

"While approaching a herd of about fifty buffalo, I inadvertantly disturbed two solitary animals on the opposite side of my car. They were about to enter a mudhole. I reversed my car to a safe distance hoping they would return, which they did. I was then able to photograph them from about nine metres as they sank into their wallow."

● *Nikon F 801 with 300mm lens; bean bag; f5.6 at 1/250 sec; Kodachrome 200*

DIETMAR NILL (GERMANY)
SCOPS OWL

"This shot was taken at dawn during a marvellous stay in the Camargue, France, in May 1991. After a thorough search for scops owls I finally found a nest-hole in an old apple tree."

● *Nikon F4 with 300mm lens; flash; Fujichrome Velvia 50*

PEKKA HELO (FINLAND)
REDSHANK

"I'm a professional photographer with a special interest in birds. This redshank was photographed in Varanger, Norway. It was trying to distract attention away from its young."

● *Minolta X700 with 560mm lens; tripod; f6.8 at 1/250 sec; Kodachrome 200*

MARK INSOLE (UK)
WATTLED PLOVER (left)

"We approached a waterhole in the Masai Mara, Kenya, to observe a hyaena wallowing. When we turned the car engine off, a wattled plover appeared from out of the short grass and, totally oblivious to us, waded towards us."

● *Nikon FE2 with 300mm lens; f4.5 at 1/250 sec; Kodachrome 64*

GARY L LACKIE (USA)
BROWN BEAR

"Walking down to the falls in Katmai National Park in Alaska to photograph bears fishing, we came upon this big fellow. I set my tripod as low as possible and approached him carefully, wondering if there was enough light under the trees for the photograph. He was still quite sleepy and so he didn't seem to mind me, even though I was just 50 or 60 feet away. I always talk to the animals I work with, just as I would to my dog. It seems to calm them."

● *Canon F1n with 400mm lens; f2.8 at 1/15 sec; Fujichrome 100*

GARY L LACKIE (USA)
ATTEMPTED LAUNCH (right)

"The bear, probably a female, was walking along the bank when it saw the boat and looked into it. Then she walked over to where it was attached and started pulling on the knot. The boat would move as the bear yanked on the rope, sometimes startling her. After quite some time of worrying the knot, she gave up – with only one more turn to go."

● *Canon F1n with 400mm lens and x2 extender; tripod; f2.8 at 1/125 sec; Fujichrome 100*

FRITZ PÖLKING (GERMANY)
ELEPHANT SEAL AND TUSSACBIRD

"The tussacbird is interested in the flies to be found around the nose of the southern elephant seal. I specialise in photographing animal behaviour and was in the Falkland Islands at the time, leading a tour." Fritz Polking has an eye for the humorous – this is the third time he has won a prize in this category.

● *Nikon F4 with 300mm lens; tripod; f4 auto; Kodachrome 64*

RICHARD REVELS (UK)

NUT THIEF

"After a friend told me about a coal tit seen perching on a squirrel's chest in the RSPB reserve at Sandy, I decided to spend a day there with my camera. After about an hour in the hide, I was rewarded with this scene."

● *Canon T90 with 300mm lens and 1.4 extender; flash; Kodachrome 64*

FRANS LANTING
(THE NETHERLANDS)
AFRICAN NESSIE

"The first sighting of 'Nessie' in southern Africa! An elephant is crossing the Chobe river, which isn't very deep, so it may be walking along the bottom. Occasionally, whole herds cross this way, the cows with their little ones in between them. This was an adult bull. I used a long lens for technical reasons and also so as not to obstruct the elephant's progress and to avoid getting swamped."

CHARLIE HAMILTON JAMES (UK)
OTTERS (right)

"I watched these four otters – mother and her three cubs – every day for three weeks on Shetland. When I took the picture it was raining and I was looking down on them from halfway up a cliff. I'd probably been there for about an hour, and I think the mother knew I was there."

Charlie was Young Wildlife Photographer of the Year in 1990, and is now studying photography at Falmouth School of Art and Design. His picture of otters is also the winner of the category for 14-17 year-olds.

● *Nikon F3 with 500mm lens; bean bag; f8 at 1/30 sec; Kodachrome 200*

NICK SAYER (UK)

ROE DEER DOE

"I went out at 6am with my camera and binoculars specifically to look for deer and foxes. While walking quietly through some local woodland I surprised this roe doe. She looked attractive through the trees with the morning sun filtering on to her coat. By avoiding eye contact and acting in a relaxed and inconspicuous way I didn't worry her and I was able to take the picture."

● *Olympus OM10 with 400mm lens; monopod; f5.6; Ektachrome 200*

WINNER: 11-14 YEARS

RHIAN THOMAS (UK)

PRIMROSES (right)

"I found the primroses in some woodland near my home and decided to photograph them because they were in perfect condition and there was no wind. Also, the hazy sunshine and light cloud produced good soft light and low contrast."

● *Canon AE1 with 100mm lens; tripod; f11 at 1/30 sec; Ektachrome 64*

JOHN BROADBENT (UK)
PUFFIN (left)

"I went to Skomer hoping to take a photograph of a puffin with a beakful of sandeels. I stalked the puffin along a cliff path and waited until mid-afternoon to have the sun behind me. I don't own my own camera but my father allows me to use his." John specializes in photographing seabirds and already has had some pictures published.

● *Canon EOS600 with 50-200mm lens; polarizing filter; f5.6 at 1/500 sec; Fujichrome 100*

JAMES AKERS (UK)
THRIFT

"On holiday in Scotland, I saw some thrift growing on a rock on the beach. The rock behind was in the shadow and this made the flowers stand out. I take a lot of pictures. I always take my camera on holiday and often go out with my dad at week-ends."

● *Nikon FG20 with 55mm lens; Fujichrome 100*

REBECCA DEAN (UK)

GREEN BEE-EATER

''The bee-eater was sitting in the shade resting or waiting for a bee or beetle to pass by. The lighting was good although the bird was in the shade, and I was pleased by the way it glowed on the branch.'' Rebecca took her winning shot while on a birdwatching holiday in Sri Lanka.

● *Olympus OM2n with 100-300mm lens; f8 at 1/125 sec; Kodachrome 200*

Bob Talbot

BBC WILDLIFE IS BRITAIN'S BEST-SELLING MONTHLY MAGAZINE ON WILDLIFE AND THE ENVIRONMENT

We *take pride in publishing the world's best wildlife images*

THE NATURAL HISTORY MUSEUM
South Kensington, London

Across the world, the name of The Natural History Museum is synonymous with dinosaurs. But behind the Museum's Victorian facade is a highly complex and sophisticated modern scientific centre.

Without a doubt the dinosaurs will always be a great attraction. This is illustrated by the popularity of the massive new dinosaur exhibition of ancient skeletons and life-size robotic models, open from April 1992. The exhibition asks whether dinosaurs resembled today's animals – did they care for their young, were they hot- or cold-blooded, and why did they die out? This is in line with all the latest interactive exhibitions, which tackle topical processes of nature such as ecology, evolution and human biology. Also on display are collections of animals, plants, fossils, minerals, rocks and meteorites, providing a dazzling display of the natural world.

The Museum is the home of the nation's natural history collections, which have grown from its origin in 1753 to a current total of over 67 million specimens, 1 million books and many original drawings, prints and paintings.

Unknown to the millions of people that visit each year, there are over 300 scientists working behind the scenes. They have access to an unrivalled fund of data on the natural world against which ecological and geological change can be measured. Every day, these scientists are addressing vital environmental issues such as loss of natural habitats and biological diversity, and the effects of global warming. They are also fighting deadly insect-borne diseases such as bilharzia, which affects at least 200 million people throughout the tropics.

The strength of the Museum's science makes it a leading international institution for the identification and classification of the natural world. Its award-winning displays capture the imagination of visitors of all ages, offering them an enjoyable way to learn. The Natural History Museum is rightly called the home of natural history.

PHOTOGRAPHERS' INDEX

The numbers set in italic type after the photographer's name indicate the pages on which their work can be found.

James **AKERS** (UK) *149*

Karl **AMMAN** (Switzerland) *69*
Box 39446
Nairobi
Kenya

Tel: 0176 22448
Fax: 0176 22145

Uwe **ANDERS** (Germany) *79*
Mariemstrasse 1
3300 Braunschweig
Germany

Tel: 0531 796535

Andre **BÄRTSCHI** (Liechtenstein) *93*
Bannholzstrasse 10
FL-9490 Vaduz
Liechtenstein

Tel: 075 203 38
Fax: 075 203 39

Erwin & Peggy **BAUER** (USA) *96*
Wildstock
P.O. Box 987
Livingston
Montana 59047
USA

Tel: (406) 222 7100

Rajesh **BEDI** (India) *11*
Bedi Films
E-19 Rajouri Gardens
New Delhi 110027
India

Andy **BELCHER** (New Zealand) *111*
Creative Underwater Photography
81 Percy Road
Papamoa
Tauranga
New Zealand

Tel: 07 5420 419

Jim **BRANDENBURG** (USA) *12*

Agent:
Minden Pictures
119-A Marina Avenue
Aptos
CA 95003
USA

Tel: (408) 685 1911
Fax: (408) 685 1913

John **BROADBENT** (UK) *148*
22 Sycamore Crescent
Barry
S. Glamorgan
CF6 7DW

Tel: 0446 740362
Fax: c/o Peter Broadbent
        0446 745979

Bela **BERTA** (Hungary) *73*
Csobogos U.4.X/63
H-1151 Budapest
Hungary

Scott **CAMAZINE** (USA) *81*
36 Dove Drive
Ithaca
NY 14850
USA

Tel: (607) 272 2512 (Home)
        (607) 255 6574 (Office)
Fax: (607) 255 8088

Allen **CAMPBELL** (USA) *110*
122 N. Main Street
Henderson
KY 42420
USA

Tel: (502) 826 9912
Fax: (502) 827 9913

Laurie **CAMPBELL** (UK) *48*
30 Blinkbonny
Currie
Midlothian EH14 6AE
Scotland

George S. K. **CHIEW** (Malaysia) *107*
83 Flushing Garden
Kenyalang Park
93300 Kuching
Sarawak
Malaysia

Tel: Malaysia 082 243881 (Home)
        Malaysia 082 413642 (Office)
Fax: Malaysia 082 427859

Judd **COONEY** (USA) *47*
Box 808
Pagosa Springs
Co. 81147
USA

Tel: (303) 264 5612

Gordon **COURT** (New Zealand) *65*
Department of Zoology
University of Otago
Dunedin
New Zealand

Tel: NZ 03 479 7986
Fax: NZ 03 479 7584

Daniel J. **COX** (USA) *54, 57, 104*
16595 Brackett Creek Road
Bozeman
Montana 59915
USA

Tel: (406) 686 4448
Fax: (406) 686 4448

Peter Bárdos **DEAK** (Hungary) *74*
Szölö-Köz 7 IV em 12
1032 Budapest
Hungary

Rebecca **DEAN** (UK) *150*

Gertrud & Helmut **DENZAU** (Germany) *49*
Memelstrasse 61
D-4300 Essen 15
Germany

Tel: 0201 465188

Monika **DUSCHER** (Austria) *135*
50 Cambridge Gardens
Flat 0
London W10 5UD

Natalino **FENECH** (Malta) *88*
35 Main Street
Attard
Malta

Steven **FULLER** (USA) *108, 122,*
        Endpapers
P.O. Box 524
Yellowstone Park
Wyoming 82190
USA

Nick **GARBUTT** (UK) *119*
c/o 30 School Road
Wales
Sheffield S31 8QJ
S. Yorks

Tel: 0909 770954

Mike **GILLAM** (Australia) *80*
P.O. Box 3435
Alice Springs
Northern Territory 0871
Australia

Tel: 089 534211

Chris **GILLMAN** (New Zealand) *87*
51 Heriot Row
Dunedin
New Zealand

Bob **GLOVER** (UK) *55*
Hedge Hills
Etheldor Avenue
Hockley
Essex

Tel: 0702 201959

Dr Roger **GRACE** (New Zealand) *89*
P.O. Box 12-012
Penrose
Auckland 5
New Zealand

Tel: 0 9 5798 498

Janet **HAAS** (USA) *58*
P.O. Box 174
Milford
Michigan 48381
USA

Jean Francois **HELLIO** (France) *68, 76*
& Nicholas van Ingen
Le Pied du Tour
36800 Minge
France

Tel: 54 37 86 65
Fax: 54 37 87 61

Pekka **HELO** (Finland) *139*
Tilhitie 7
87400 Kajaani 40
Finland

Richard **HERRMANN** Photrography (USA) *112, 121*
12545 Mustang Drive
Poway
California 92064
USA

Tel: (619) 679 7017

Lex **HES** (South Africa) *125*
P.O. Box 6
Skukuza 1350
South Africa

Tel: 01311 65653
Fax: 01311 65100

John & Karen **HOLLINGSWORTH** (USA) *118*
Reflections of Nature
12137 Rist Canyon Road
Bellvue
Colorado 80512
USA

Nicholas van **INGEN** (France) *68, 76*
& Jean Francois Hellio
Le Pied du Tour
36800 Minge
France

Tel: 54 37 86 65
Fax: 54 37 87 61

Mark **INSOLE** (UK) *139*
Garden Flat
80 Pembroke Road
Bristol BS8 3EG

Tel: 0272 736584

Charlie Hamilton **JAMES** (UK) *145*
20 Cotham Park
Cotham
Bristol
BS6 6BU

Tel: (0272) 249397

Jan Tõve **JOHANSSON** (Sweden) *103*
Prästgården Härna
520 15 Hokerum
Sweden

Tel: 033 74028

Bert **JONES** & Maurine Shimlock (USA) *21, 22, 23, 24, 25, 26, 27, 28*
P.O. Box 162931
Austin
Texas 78716
USA

Tel: (512) 328 1201

Hans Christoph **KAPPEL** (Germany) *73, 77*
Hugo-Preuss Strasse 32
D-3500 Kassel
Germany

Tel: (0561) 31 39 43

Agent
W.WF-Archiv
Bahronfelder Strasse 242
D-2000 Hamburg 50
Germany

Pam **KEMP** (UK) *85*
12 Prospero House
Essenden Road
Belvedere
Kent DA17 5ED

Richard & Julia **KEMP** (UK) *9*
South Cottage
Deopham
Wymondham
Norfolk NR18 9DU

Tel: (0953) 850688

Rich **KIRCHNER** (USA) *Jacket, 52, 132, 136*
P.O. Box 1261
Bozeman
Montana 59715
USA

Tel: (406) 587 3275

Chris **KNIGHTS** (UK) *82*
Crow Hall Farm
Gooderstone
Kings Lynn
Norfolk PF33 9DA

Tel: 036621 646
Fax: 036621 746

Garry **LACKIE** (USA) *140, 141*
P.O. Box 110405
Anchorage
Alaska 99511
USA

Gordon **LANGSBURY** (UK) *70*
80 Shepherds Close
Hurley
Maidenhead
SL6 5LZ

Tel: 0628 824252

Frans **LANTING** (The Netherlands) *15, 16, 17, 18, 19, 20, 67, 101, 131, 144*

Agent:
Minden Pictures
119-A Marina Avenue
Aptos
CA 95003
USA

Tel: (408) 685 1911
Fax: (408) 685 1913

Antii **LEINONEN** (Finland) 95
Torikatu 27
88900 Kuhmo
Finland

Tel: 986 51775

Martin **LILLICRAP** (UK) 120
24B Avonale Road
Wealdstone
Harrow
Middlesex HA3 7RE

Tel: 081 863 8037

Luiz Claudio **MARIGO** (Brazil) 80
Rua Leitao da Cunha
48/302-Laranjeiras
22251-Rio de Janeiro
Brazil

Tel: (021) 285 4606
Fax: (021) 556 1832

Francisco **MARQUEZ** (Spain) 53, 98
Avda. Fco. Aguirre 230
45600 Talavera de la Reina
Toledo
Spain

Tel: (925) 803977

Mark **MATTOCK** (UK) 81, 119, 120
19 Lambourne Close
Ledbury
Herefordshire

Agent:
Planet Earth Pictures
4 Harcourt Street
London W1H 1DS

Tel: 071 262 4427
Fax: 071 706 4042

Lennart **MELLGREN** (Sweden) 71
Bergstigen 7
S-46832 Vargon
Sweden

Tel: 0521 20918

Stefan **MEYERS** (Germany) 45
Berchenstrasse 38
D-7750 Konstanz
Germany

Sunjoy **MONGA** (India) 94
45/46 Madhurima
M.G. Road
Kandiuli (West)
Bombay 400-067
India

Tel: 605 2148
606 3992

Jussi **MURTOSAARI** (Finland) 59
Tyyppalantie 2 D 29
40250 Jyväskylä
Finland

Tel: 941 685 045

Vincent **McGOLDRICK** (UK) 86
7 Queensbrae
Carryduff
Co. Antrim
Northern Ireland

Tel: 0232 812565

Neil **McINTYRE** (UK) 37, 38, 39, 40,
41, 42, 43, 44
The Kennels
Kinrara
Aviemore
PH 22 1QA
Scotland

Tel: 0479 810713

Rick **McINTYRE** (USA) 51
Summer Address (June/September)
Many Glacier Ranger Station
Box 90 Babb
MT. 59411
USA

Tel: (406) 732 5586

Winter address (Oct/May)
Cottonwood Ranger Station
Chiriaco Summit
CA 92201
USA

Tel: (619) 367 7511

Terry **NEWMAN** (UK) 117
4 Trevale
Tredarvah
Penzance
Cornwall TR18 4JJ

Tel: 0736 64704

Pauli **NIEMINEN** (Finland) 123
Honkaniemi
02440 Luoma
Finland

Dietmar **NILL** (Germany) 138
Schönbergstrasse 44
7406 Mössingen-Oschingen
Germany

Tel: 07473 21121

Boyd **NORTON** (USA) 130
P.O. Box 2605
Evergreen
Colorado 80439
USA

David **NOTON** (UK) 105, 128
20 Doone Road
Horfield
Bristol BS7 0JG

Tel: 0272 512489

Ben **OSBORNE** (UK) 134
Sunningdale
Pontesford Hill
Pontesbury
Shrewsbury SY5 0UN

Tel: 0743 790165

Agent:
Oxford Scientific Films
Long Hanborough
Nr. Oxford OX7 2LD

Tel: 0993 881881
Fax: 0993 882808

Michael **OSMOND** (Australia) 116
P.O. Box 324
North Beach 6020
Western Australia

Tel: 9 448 5800 (Office)
9 387 2435 (Home)
Fax: 9 447 8713

Dr Jeremy P. **OWEN** (UK) 116
c/o 'St. Davids'
Hartle Lane
Belbroughton
Nr. Stourbridge
West Midlands DY9 9TJ

Richard **PACKWOOD** (UK) 90
22 The Gardens
Kerry
Newtown
Powys
Wales

Tel: 068688 700

William S. **PATON** (UK) 137
74 Portland Street
Kilmarnock
Ayrshire
KA3 1AA
Scotland

Tel: 0563 26273

Jorma **PEIPONEN** (Finland) *108*
Alakiri Ibio
40630 Jyraskyla
Finland

Tel: 941 245693

Risto **PETÄ JÄMÄKI** (Finland) *64*
Pihlajankaari 15
54100 Joutseno
Finland

Tel: 953 33257

Linda **PITKIN** (UK) *113, 114*
12 Coningsby Road
South Croydon
Surrey CR2 6QP

Tel: 081 668 8168

Agent:
Planet Earth Pictures
4 Harcourt Street
London WA6 1DS

Tel: 071 262 4427

Fritz **PÖLKING** (Germany) *142*
Münsterstrasse 71
D-4402 Greven
Germany

Tel: 02571 52115
Fax: 02571 6026

Benjam **PÖNTINEN** (Finland) *63*
Onnelantie 9
60550 Nurmo
Finland

Tel: 358 64 146136

Allan G. **POTTS** (UK) *106*
Nature World Productions
East Farm
Backworth
Newcastle-upon-Tyne
NE27 0AL

Tel: 268 4706

Glen **PRATT** (USA) *56*
P.O. Box 520166
Big Lake
Alaska 99652
USA

Colin **PRIOR** (UK) *91*
Environmental/Panoramic Photography

Tel: 0698 818131
Fax: 0698 815257
Mobile: 0836 357595

Picture Library
Tony Stone Worldwide

Tel: 071 267 8988
Fax: 071 722 9305

Helmut **PUM** (Austria) *62*
Vuchholzer str. 9
A-4400 Speyr
Austria

A. K. **RAJU** (India) *99*
Engineering Copies
"Hariram Complex"
34 K.G. ROAD
Bangalore 560009
India

Dr Morley **READ** (UK) *89*
Readymoney Cove
Fowey
Cornwall PL23 1JH

Also:
Casilla 344A
Surcursal 3, Ulloa Y Ramirez Davilos
Quito
Ecuador

Tel: 546480
Fax: 568664

Benoit **RENEVEY** (Switzerland) *66*
Villette 13
CH-1400 Yverdon-les-Bains
Switzerland

Tel: (024) 21 80 84

Richard **REVELS** (UK) *143*
Photo Library
73 London Road
Biggleswade
Beds SG18 8EE

Dave **ROBINSON** (UK) *97*
Meadowside
15 Grimpits Lane
Wythall
Nr. Birmingham B38 9EY

Norbert **ROSING** (Germany) *60*
Amselweg 15
D-8082 Grafrath
Germany

Tel: (49) 8144 7813
Fax: (49) 8143 7374

Jeffrey L. **ROTMAN** (USA) *109, 124,*
   125
14 Cottage Avenue
Somerville
Mass. 02144
USA

Tel: (617) 666 0874
Fax: (617) 666 4811

Jouni **RUUSKANEN** (Finland) *13*
Teerikatu 3 B 15
87500 Kajaani
Finland

Tel: 358 86 25751 (Office)
   358 86 140424 (Home)

Alain **SAUNIER** (Switzerland) *46*
Photo Nature
CH-2745 Grandval
Switzerland

Tel: 032 93 97 73

Nick **SAYER** (UK) *146*

Erling **SCHON** (Sweden) *83*
Råhusgatan 9A
52335 Ütriochamn
Sweden

Tel: 0321 14989

Jonathan **SCOTT** (UK) *11*
Planet Earth Pictures
4 Harcourt Street
London W1H 1DS

Tel: 071 262 4427
Fax: 071 706 4042

Wendy **SHATTIL** (USA) *14*
P.O. Box 37422
Denver
Colorado 80237
USA

Tel: (303) 721 1991
Fax: (303) 721 1116

Yuri **SHIBNEV** (USSR) *78*
692710 Primorskiy Krai
Khasanskiy Raion
Pos. Primorskiy
Kedrovajapad Nature Reserve
USSR

Maurine **SHIMLOCK** & Bert Jones (USA)
21, 22, 23, 24, 25, 26, 27, 28
P.O. Box 162931
Austin
Texas 78716
USA

Tel: 512 328 1201

Gabriele **SOMENZI** (Italy) *84*
Via G. Verdi 37
Poveromo
Massa 54039
Italy

Tel: 010 39 585 241449

Claude **STEELMAN** (USA) *133*
Wildshots
P.O. Box 2527
Durango
Colorado 81302
USA

Tel: (303) 259 5202

Charles G. **SUMMERS**, Jr. (USA) *10*
Colorado Nature Photos
6392 S. Yellowstone Way
Aurora
Colorado 80016
USA

Tel: (303) 690 5532
Fax: (303) 693 4750

Paul **TAYLOR** (UK) *75, 102*
Fieldwork Photography
Catchwater Farm
Butterwick Road
Messingham
South Humberside DN17 3PL

Tel: 0724 763081

Rhian **THOMAS** (UK) *147*

Darryl **TORCKLER** (New Zealand) *115*
P.O. Box 33693
Takapuna
Auckland 9
New Zealand

Tel: 09 478 9230
Fax: 09 479 2214

Bobby **TULLOCH** (UK) *126*
Lüsetter
Mid Yisll
Shetland ZE2 9BN
Scotland

Tel: (0957) 2226

Jeff **VANUGA** (USA) *72*
P.O. Box 1450
1428 Highview
Dubois
Wyoming 82513
USA

Tel: (307) 455 2194
Fax: (307) 455 2567

Kennan **WARD** Photography *88, 100*
P.O. Box 42
Santa Cruz
CA 95063
USA

Tel: (408) 429 9533

John **WARDEN** (USA) *50 129*
Warden & Associates
9201 Shorecrest Drive
Anchorage
AK 99515
USA

Tel: (907) 243 1667

Lev **WEISMAN/ANA** (USSR) *61*
6 Avenue Reny Coty
75014 Paris
France

Tel: 43 22 62 11
Fax: 43 35 28 38

Martin **WENDLER** (Germany) *92*
Schwarzbrunnenstrasse 10
8901 Welden
Germany

Tel: 08293 1049

Kim **WESTERSKOV** (New Zealand) *127*
Natural Images
72 Emmett Street
Tauranga
New Zealand

Tel: 07 578 5138

Konrad **WOTHE** (Germany) *29, 30, 31,
32, 33, 34, 35, 36, 57*
Konrad-Witz-Strasse 15
8000 Munich 71
Germany

Tel: 089 798675

The Wildlife Photographer of the Year Competition is an annual event. Entry forms for the 1992 competition can be found in the spring issues of BBC WILDLIFE Magazine. Overseas photographers can write for further details to: Wildlife Photographer of the Year Competition c/o BBC WILDLIFE Magazine Broadcasting House Whiteladies Road Bristol BS8 2LR